Effective
Reading Instruction
For Slow Learners

Effective
Reading Instruction
For Slow Learners

By

DONALD C. CUSHENBERY, Ed.D.

Foundation Professor of Education
Director, Reading Clinic
University of Nebraska at Omaha
Omaha, Nebraska

and

KENNETH J. GILREATH, M.S.

Assistant Professor of Education
University of Nebraska at Omaha
Omaha, Nebraska

CHARLES C THOMAS • PUBLISHER
Springfield • Illinois • U.S.A.

Published and Distributed Throughout the World by

CHARLES C THOMAS • PUBLISHER

BANNERSTONE HOUSE

301–327 East Lawrence Avenue, Springfield, Illinois, U.S.A.

© *1972, by* CHARLES C THOMAS • PUBLISHER

ISBN 0–398–02543–6

Library of Congress Catalog Card Number: 72–75914

With THOMAS BOOKS *careful attention is given to all details of manufacturing and design. It is the Publisher's desire to present books that are satisfactory as to their physical qualities and artistic possibilities and appropriate for their particular use. THOMAS BOOKS will be true to those laws of quality that assure a good name and good will.*

Printed in the United States of America

GG–11

PREFACE

The importance of reading as a body of skills to be developed by all children has been a point of emphasis on the part of all educators since the inception of public and private educational systems. Children who cannot read properly are discriminated against in varying degrees by their peers and society in general.

Though much success has been attained in recent years in the construction and promotion of reading programs for the so-called normal child, there is a significant vacuum in the number of practical, professional helps available for meeting the reading needs of the slow learner. Because of the numerous requests from teachers for assistance in this area, we have constructed this volume for *all* teachers who deal with the slow learner. The suggestions contained in the materials have been classroom-tested for use in the regular heterogeneous class as well as in the special educable and/or mentally handicapped classes.

Appropriate references have been included at the close of each chapter for those readers who wish to read additional volumes for amplifications of specific subjects. The appendices contain a wealth of ideas with respect to the use of commercial materials. Prices have not been included in most instances, since this information is subject to frequent change. Publishers' addresses have been included in a separate appendix.

Chapter I contains a description of the slow learner with respect to his basic characteristics and educational and psychological needs. The need for building a broad, inclusive developmental program for the slow learner is explored in Chapter II. The first phase of the reading act, reading readiness, is explained in Chapter III, along with a description of many practical teaching suggestions for promoting this learning level. Chapter IV consists of a discussion of the general program of reading evaluation as it applies to the slow learner. The core of the reading act, word analysis, with all of its major ramifications, is explained in Chapter V. In Chapter VI, a complete description of the methods available for building comprehension skills is included.

Since slow-learning children are very often limited in the area of perceptual-motor abilities, a discussion of practical procedures for building these skills is described in Chapter VII. Because one of the most important keys to reading success is motivation, a selected list of useful teaching plans is contained in Chapter VIII. Chapter IX consists of an extensive description of many commercial materials which are available for use with the slow learner.

The topics in this volume were chosen after a careful study was conducted of the many requests from teachers of slow learners for classroom help in building reading skills. We have reason to believe that hundreds of other teachers have similar desires and are in a position to make use of the valuable aids contained in this volume.

ACKNOWLEDGMENTS

The authors wish to acknowledge their indebtedness to the faculty and staff of the Department of Special Education, University of Nebraska at Omaha, for their constant encouragement while the manuscript was in the process of preparation.

We also wish to express our appreciation to Mrs. Norma Johnson, Mrs. Bonnie Abboud, Miss Linda Joern, and Miss Gail Rinehart for their help in the preparation of the appendices section and for proofreading the manuscript at various stages.

Our gratitude is extended to Mrs. Edwin K. Wright, the manuscript typist, for her patience and thoroughness. Professor Phillip Smith, Department of English, University of Nebraska at Omaha, served as the official proofreader, and we are indebted to him for his constructive criticisms.

Many teachers of slow-learning children encouraged us to compile the manuscript. Some of the classroom-tested practices which are described in the volume have been supplied by outstanding teachers in the Omaha area, and to these educators we express our sincere thanks.

A volume of this nature consumed an enormous amount of time and research which has been subtracted from the hours which might have been spent with our families. To our wives and children, we express our deepest appreciation for their understanding and helpful attitudes.

D.C.C.
K.J.G.

CONTENTS

Effective
Reading Instruction
For Slow Learners

Chapter I

DESCRIBING THE SLOW LEARNER

Kenneth J. Gilreath

It should be pointed out at the beginning that the generally accepted meaning of the term "slow learner" is not exactly what is meant in the context of this volume. While it is true that the term is widely used in educational circles to refer to students who fall in the range of 75 to 90 IQ on the *Stanford-Binet* and other commonly used psychological tests, it is also true that there are many other students in our schools who fail to keep pace with their peers in academic achievement. This group could, and quite obviously should, include those children who, for whatever reasons, are experiencing difficulty in school. The educable mentally retarded (EMR), the socially maladjusted, the emotionally disturbed, and the culturally disadvantaged are all labels which are known to all of us and should be included when we consider how we can best serve these children educationally.

In order to understand the slow learner in the classroom, a description of the various kinds of learning problems that confront the teacher is in order. This chapter will serve to introduce the kinds of problems commonly found in children who are not learning as rapidly as they should.

THE EDUCABLE MENTALLY RETARDED CHILD

The causes of mental retardation are varied, but they might generally be traced to two major areas which are often intermingled so that they become difficult to separate. They are (a) heredity, the mental ability which is genetically controlled and (b) environment, the intellectual limitations imposed by one's surroundings. This cultural-familial retardation affects a very large percentage of our slow-learning population. It is important that teachers recognize these causative factors and understand that it is not an "either-or" proposition.

Intelligence can be identified in two ways; the first being *inference*, the basic capacity of an individual to learn. This would be his hereditary potential, and under ideal educational, environmental, and psychological conditions, the child would be able to achieve this intellectual potential. The second level of identifying intelligence is *measure*, the operational level at which the child is currently functioning. Assuming that adequate tests are used by competent testers under satisfactory testing conditions, a gap often exists between the inferred or potential intelligence of a child and the functional or operational level of intelligence. In the case of the culturally disadvantaged child, this gap is greater than it is in the case of the child who is meeting success in the classroom.

The gap that exists between what the cultural, familially retarded child *can* achieve and what he *is* achieving is caused primarily by environmental factors that are affecting him both at home and in school. This child usually has difficulty in school almost from the beginning. He lacks the background of experience that is so necessary for academic success, and this type of weakness is most apparent in reading, where he seems to have the greatest difficulty.

Learning Problems of EMR Pupils

The educable mentally retarded child displays some specific learning problems. It is important for a teacher to be aware of these problems if she is to guide the child effectively in school.

First, the EMR child learns more slowly than the average child. The problem of late maturation, readiness, and motivation all contribute to this area of difficulty. While studies have indicated that mentally handicapped students learn as rapidly as normal children of the same mental age, it should be pointed out that over a long period of time, the retarded child will fall behind. In one year, for example, a normal 9-year-old child will gain one year in mental age, whereas a retarded 12-year-old (mental age 9) will grow only three-fourths of a year. This means that the EMR child will have a mental age of 9 years and 7 months. Quite obviously, then, the normal child does learn more rapidly than the slow learner.

Studies by Vergasen,[1] Heber,[2] and others indicate that while it is true that learning is slower, specific methods can compensate for this failure.

Second, the EMR child retains information less efficiently than does a normal child. The many studies that have been done to verify this fact also indicate that proper teaching techniques (such as drills designed to achieve overlearning) can do much to correct this weakness.

Another learning problem is that the EMR child has a great deal of difficulty in transferring information. A good example of what is meant is the child's inability to apply a simple mathematical concept learned in numerical form to a similar problem dealing with budgeting of money. Teachers have learned that by making their lessons practical and concrete, they can assist the child in compensating for this weakness.

It has been observed that a child can learn to tell time quite efficiently by using the paper-plate clock his teacher has constructed for him. He will, however, probably not be able to transfer this knowledge to the school clock on the wall or to the wrist-watch which his parents have rewarded him for his "time-telling" achievement.

Finally, the slow-learning child suffers from what might best be described as an overreaction to failure. It has long been a practice of teachers throughout the country to fail children who do not come up to their expectation or to the level of the class. Some believe that this practice is motivating to the student. Evidence seems quite clear, however, that failure has the opposite effect on the slow learner. Gardner[3] used an electronically controlled device to measure students' reactions to failure. The device consisted of a magnetic track which was graduated, a metal ball, and a bulb. The students were told that the harder they squeezed the bulb, the higher the ball would go up the scale. The child was asked to predict the level to which he would make the ball go. This was identified as the *level of expectancy*. The height to which the ball goes was identified as the *level of performance*. The apparatus was rigged in such a manner that the child was unable to reach his level of expectancy. The results of the study are included in the statements which follow. In all instances, after the first actual performance (which was controlled so that it was less than the child's aspiration), the child selected a level of aspiration which was lower than the first. The experimenter never allowed the child to reach his aspiration level no matter how low it was. Because of his continued failure, the child ultimately gave up.

The interesting part of this experiment, however, was the difference in the way the slow-learning and the normal children responded to their inability to reach their goal, e.g. expectancy level. The normal group set its level of expectancy halfway between expectancy and performance, their attitude seeming to be that with repeated effort their achievement would improve; but the slower students set their level of expectancy at their last achievement. The implication was clear that no matter how hard they tried or how much they practiced, they could not improve on their last performance. It would appear, if one accepts the study, that a failing grade or an experience where the child was not able to find success would have a debilitating effect on the slow-learning child.

Chapter VIII deals specifically with methods of identifying many of these learning problems. Regardless of whether the slow-learning child is found in a special class or in a regular class, the teacher should be well advised to consider these conditions.

THE SOCIALLY MALADJUSTED CHILD

Educators have seen profound effects of social factors on the educational process. Rapidly changing school curricula reflect this concern. It is now a common practice to find school programs providing such services as the following: (a) guidance programs on the elementary and secondary level, (b) psychological services, (c) school social workers, (d) remedial instruction and special placement, and (e) in-service and/or special training for teachers.

Though these supportive services are considered very helpful and in some cases essential to the academic success of a child, the fact remains that the classroom teacher continues to be the most influential factor in a child's achievement and satisfaction with school. It should also be pointed out that in some cases of severe behavioral stress, even the abovementioned services are not sufficient to allow a child to remain in school. Society in general and schools in particular have become more and more concerned with the problem of social maladjustment. The rapid increase in juvenile crime has served to make the problem even more immediate. Another factor which has given impetus to educational action has been the trend of the school to address itself to more and more of society's problems.

Definition

The socially maladjusted child is one who refuses to comply with the rules of society and school. He defies the teacher, disrupts the class, and threatens and abuses his classmates. This kind of child generally displays behavior which interferes with his individual growth, as well as that of others. His notoriety is passed up the line from teacher to teacher along with his cumulative folder. This file bulges with anecdotes of antisocial and "antischool" behavior. He is the child that every teacher, every principal, and every school counselor remembers. Perhaps the most important fact about this child is that *he is unsuccessful in school*. Like many other unsuccessful students, he faces major educational problems in the field of reading.

One should remember that social maladjustment and emotional disturbance are substantially different terms. While there is overlapping between the two, some differentiation can be made. Social maladjustment is considered a social problem, while emotional disturbance is thought of as psychological in nature. Another difference that is easily recognizable is that the socially maladjusted youngster violates the law frequently. His defiance of civil and school law often serves to win favor from his peer group, while the emotionally disturbed child seldom is capable of behavior which is accepted in the complicated structure of the gang society.

Learning Problems of the Socially Maladjusted Child

The learning problems which confront this group of individuals most often fall in the area of motivation. The curriculum of most classrooms fails to interest these children, and the structure of the classroom is not designed to meet their needs. If teachers are to be successful in reaching the behaviorally deviant child, they must be willing to make considerable changes in several areas.

The basic problem of these pupils is a combination of low ability and a narrow range of interests. The course content must be adjusted in such a fashion as to not only interest the child but to adjust to his level of ability as well. This type of student is usually deficient in vocabulary and skills due to his history of antisocial behavior and his lack of interest in the material that has been used in the past. The effective teacher should be aware of the need to present special materials which will give the child an opportunity to succeed.

Teaching methods which are successful with normal children often fail with the socially maladjusted child. The personal rewards of academic success and teacher approval are simply not important to him. Threats of punishment, such as parental conferences or expulsion from class or school, and withholding of any kind of adult approval lack effectiveness in motivating these socially maladjusted children. Perhaps the most effective technique in dealing with them is through their peer group association. The effective teacher will approach the problem of acceptable social behavior in a manner which will allow the child to succeed in school by meeting its social standards. At the same time, the demands of his peer group or gang can be satisfied, thus making it possible for the child to remain in school, benefit from the academic program, and continue to function within the social stratum in which he finds himself.

These conditions represent a rather large order for the classroom teacher to fill. The purpose of this book is to offer practical suggestions to meet these and other learning problems which are so common in every classroom. Chapter VIII offers some practical suggestions for adapting methodology and curriculum to assist children who are socially maladjusted.

THE EMOTIONALLY DISTURBED CHILD

The number of school-age children who are affected by mental or emotional disturbance varies a great deal and depends upon which expert is quoted and what criteria of evaluation is applied. Some authorities believe that one student out of every ten is in need of psychiatric assistance. Not all of these children are found in our special or regular classrooms because of the degree of difficulty of their problem. Many of them suffer from difficulties that are so severe that school attendance is impossible. Our purpose is not to offer a discussion of the psychological or psychiatric problems of these children, but rather to offer suggestions to educators with pupils who are in school and are in academic difficulty because of emotional problems.

The education of emotionally disturbed children is a relatively new field and one in which educators often find themselves floundering. New programs, such as Head Start and the various government-sponsored compensatory education activities, are making inroads in assisting many of these children. An awareness and acceptance of the responsibilities for educating these children by both the public and the educational system has given us a start in the direction of solving the problem.

Definition

Almost all persons live in the primary social systems of the society. As one grows older, work and political agencies come more into the picture and a person learns to function fairly adequately in these situations. Therefore, the manner in which children behave must be interpreted in terms of the interaction of the child and his environment. Children who are emotionally disturbed have difficulty with other people: teachers, peers, authority figures, and siblings. They are unhappy with themselves and are unable to apply themselves to tasks in a manner which will achieve the success their ability predicts.

Educators are constantly faced with decisions that pit the welfare of one student against those of the group. Johnny's behavior disrupts the rest of the class. Should he be removed from the room or will the benefits he derives from school offset the harm to the other students? Is the extra stress he places on the teacher sufficient cause for removal? Would he gain more if he would be placed in a special class or in an institutional program? While these are questions which must be answered by the educator, the decision should reflect the professional advice of the specialist in the field of mental health.

Emotional disturbance can often be identified in children by careful observation on the part of the teacher. The inner tensions, stress, and frustration often show themselves in various forms of bizarre behavior. The teacher should be alert to the following factors:

1. Physical symptoms.
    a. Stuttering.
    b. Facial twitching.
    c. Restlessness.
    d. Foot and finger tapping.

   e. Nail biting.
2. Behavioral symptoms.
   a. Negativism.
   b. Aggressiveness.
   c. Regressiveness.
   d. Hostility.
   e. Withdrawal.
   f. Poor schoolwork.
3. Emotional maladjustment.
   a. Substitute fears.
   b. Feelings of inferiority.
   c. Pouting.
   d. Resentfulness.

Learning Problems of the Emotionally Disturbed Child

As was stated previously, it is not the intention of this book to deal with the extreme conditions of emotional disturbance. Children who suffer from severe cases of psychosis, autism, psychoneurosis, and personality disorders are seldom found in the classroom.

The learning problems of the less seriously affected emotionally disturbed children are many and varied. Because of the physical and behavioral characteristics present, these children are faced with a serious problem of attention, adequacy, and security. A good example might be taken from the traditional concept that all first graders are expected to learn to read. Reading specialists know that many 6-year-olds are not ready to read. The stresses and anxieties that result from this lack of readiness are often sufficient to adversely affect the future academic success of those students who are "tried but found wanting."

The normal activity in a classroom is another hurdle that faces the emotionally disturbed child. The necessary noise and distraction of students sharpening pencils, teachers assigning work, writing on chalkboard, and separate reading groups, etc., can be tolerated by the normal learner. This same commotion may stimulate the emotionally disturbed youngster beyond his control.

The alert teacher must learn to recognize signs of emotional problems in her students. Once spotted, she can devise course content, adapt physical surroundings, and devise teaching methods which will aid the child in controlling his behavior and enable him to function satisfactorily within the confines of the classroom.

THE DISADVANTAGED CHILD

Terms such as "culturally deprived," "slow learners," "academically retarded," "mentally retarded," and "problem children" are often used interchangeably to identify any number of children who are experiencing difficulty in school. Perhaps the pupil most often referred to is the child identified as the disadvantaged. This child is recognized as coming from a low socioeconomic class family. This group often faces problems of unemployment, underemployment, low annual income, poor housing, welfare dependency, high crime rate, and broken homes.

The educational characteristics of the disadvantaged are even more critical. They generally are deficient in language development, display a resigned attitude of hopelessness, and are academically retarded. The living conditions existent in the child's background fail to provide the experiences and stimuli necessary for developing school readiness. When the child begins school, he enters a very foreign environment and one in which it is difficult, if not impossible, for him to function.

If a child fails to learn to read in the first few years of his schooling, he will experience considerable difficulty in achieving success in other school subjects. It is imperative, therefore, that we adapt our educational program in such a fashion as to make it possible for these children to succeed.

Definition

Most experts describe rather than define the disadvantaged child. The Office of Economic Opportunity at one time defined the disadvantaged as one who comes from a family with a total annual income of under 3,000 dollars. It is apparent, however, that due to the great cost-of-living variance in our country, this definition is less than satisfactory. From my point of view, the disadvantaged are those persons who, because of factors such as substandard housing, level of education, and unemployment, are unable to attain the benefits of life which are enjoyed by the average citizen.

Learning Problems of the Disadvantaged Child

A description of the characteristics existent that adversely affect the educational success of these children might prove helpful.

1. *Language problems.* The disadvantaged child often experiences difficulty with vocabulary as well as with the abstractions and complexities of form.
2. *Speech problems.* Foreign or regional dialects isolate them. Standard "school English" is, for many, a second language.
3. *Motivational problems.* Often the disadvantaged student comes from a lifestyle that demands immediate reinforcement rather than the ability to wait for the future reward of report cards.
4. *A poor self-concept.* The child feels himself a failure and much of the typical school and teacher atmosphere reinforces this self-image.
5. *Low aspiration.* The value of school and knowledge are not considered important.
6. *Poor adult models.* The child has no appropriate adult associates.

Quite obviously, not all deprived children display all of the above-mentioned characteristics and certainly the low economic conditions of a child's home is not, in all instances, an insurmountable educational handicap.

The effects of low socioeconomic status on a child in the educational setting is generally evident at the time he enters school. Unless these conditions are dealt with effectively, they will continue to handicap the child as he continues through school. The teacher who is genuinely interested in assisting the disadvantaged child to overcome these problems will want to take advantage of his unique strengths. Most of these children do not suffer from being overprotected and thus may display the ability to handle difficult and new situations. These and other traits tend to win respect for them from their peers.

The overwhelming numbers in this group of slow learners make them a very important part of the body of problem learners. Education must take early steps in making the necessary changes, both in school and in the child, that will compensate his weaknesses and utilize his strengths. Concentrated effort to improve his self-concept and to direct his motivational ability toward achieving worthwhile goals are vitally important if this student is to succeed. It is also important that the child be guided to new concepts of thinking relating to the world of work and his own role in society.

By developing proper course content and effective ways of presenting it, the successful teacher will do much to improve the chances of success for the disadvantaged student.

SUMMARY

To summarize, in our school systems the regular classrooms as well as the special classrooms, contain many different kinds of slow learners. These children who are unable to keep pace with the rest of their age group fall behind for a variety of reasons. Whether the student falls into the classification of the EMR, the socially maladjusted, the emotionally disturbed, or the disadvantaged, he faces educational problems, particularly in the area of reading. This situation requires special attention from the teacher and the school.

If these children are to be helped, it is necessary that teachers identify and understand their particular problems. Reading is necessary to school success. It is also vital to an individual's happiness and economic well-being. For these reasons, the concerned teacher will want to concern herself with effective teaching techniques and specially designed materials which will compensate for the slow learners' weaknesses and utilize their strengths. In this manner, the slow learner will be better able to develop healthy self-concepts and academic potential, thus enabling him to fulfill his role as a contributing member of society.

REFERENCES

1. Vergasen, G. A.: Retention in retarded and normal subjects as a function of amount of original learning. *American Journal of Mental Deficiency,* *68:*623–629, 1964.
2. Heber, R., Prehm, Nardi, and Simpson, H.R.: Learning of retarded and normal children. Paper read at American Journal of Mental Deficient meeting, New York, 1962.
3. Gardner, W. I.: *Reactions of Intellectually Normal and Retarded Boys After Experimentally Induced Failure—A Social Learning Theory Interpretation.* Ann Arbor, University Microfilms, 1958.

Chapter II

BUILDING A GENERAL BODY
OF READING SKILLS

DONALD C. CUSHENBERY

The development of effective reading skills is a must for every
child for a number of reasons. First of all, his very survival may
depend on it, since catastrophe may result if he cannot read such
signs as DO NOT ENTER or DANGER. Secondly, there are a number of
day-to-day activities which require adequate levels of reading development if a person is to function as an active citizen. One is required
to read street and highway signs, newspaper stories and advertisements, letters and notes, announcements, magazine articles, telephone directories, and legal documents such as contracts. Thirdly,
much relaxation and recreation is possible when reading because
the activity is individual and the reader can become totally involved
in the story or play which unfolds before him.

In addition to the previous items, there is the social pressure
which is exerted by both peers and parents for at least grade-level
reading ability. A child who is a retarded reader very often has a
poor self-concept and a defeatist attitude with respect to many academic pursuits. He may be the unfortunate target of socially cruel
peers who tease him about being in the "dummy" reading group,
or in a few cases, he is the object of constant criticism by parents because he cannot read as well as his older sister or brother. Further
hurt is experienced by the child when he reaches the teen-age level
and cannot read well enough to study the driver's manual and thus
fails the driver's test.

Fortunately the vast majority of pupils in today's schools attains
a satisfactory level of reading achievement, and accordingly they can
feel the pleasure of being able to read at various rates, unlock unfamiliar words, and comprehend different types of reading materials. Through the analysis of commercial and teacher-made reading

achievement tests (as well as the teacher's astute observation), they can demonstrate that they have developed competencies in the areas which are described in the next section. These goals are defensible for both the normal and slow-learning child, and every primary and intermediate teacher should see that they are a part of the instructional procedures for the school year. As indicated in the previous chapter, the slow-learning pupil accomplishes these skills at a much slower rate than the so-called "average" child. These goals should be established on a long-term basis and the instruction individualized for each pupil in relationship to his level of motivation and learning modalities.

READING GOALS FOR THE SLOW LEARNER

With respect to developmental reading skills, the slow learner should be able to demonstrate proficiency in the following areas:

1. Word analysis.
   a. Uses visual-discrimination techniques as a cue for differentiating one word from another.
   b. Listens carefully to note which words sound alike and which words sound different.
   c. Notes both initial and final consonant sounds of words and is able to reproduce them.
   d. Pronounces consonant blends appropriately.
   e. Understands the generalizations involved in recognizing and pronouncing long- and short-vowel sounds.
   f. Knows the concept of the open-syllable principle which denotes the long-vowel sounds.
   g. Makes use of the final-"e" principle. (Example: in the word "make," the "a" is long and the final "e" is silent.)
   h. Remembers that an "r," "l," or "w," at the end of a word controls the sound of the preceding vowel. (Example: the "r" controls the sound of the "a" in the word "car.")
   i. Understands that a vowel digraph consists of two medial vowels in succession, in which the first one is *usually* heard and the second one is silent. (Example: "meat" and "rain.")
   j. Recognizes the generalizations which apply in determining the hard or the soft sounds for "c" and "g."

    k. Divides multisyllabic words properly in light of the common principles taught at the elementary-school level.

2. Comprehension.

    a. Understands the importance of punctuation marks and how they influence the meaning of words, phrases, and sentences.

    b. Grasps the meaning and use of figurative language as a tool for emphasizing certain types of information.

    c. Knows the importance of topics, subtopics, and chapter headings in conveying understandings to the reader.

    d. Skims reading material to gain the main idea of a section or a chapter of a given book.

    e. Selects pertinent details which should be remembered from a reading selection.

    f. Follows directions after reading an article relating to an experiment or a do-it-yourself project.

    g. Summarizes and organizes material in a meaningful paragraph after reading a longer selection such as a magazine article.

    h. Predicts the outcome of a story after having read the background and several paragraphs of an article.

    i. Demonstrates the ability to distinguish between a fact and an opinion.

    j. Follows the plan and intent of the writer and understands why he arranged the material in a certain fashion.

    k. Reads maps, graphs, and charts, and derives significant pieces of information from such sources.

    l. Recognizes the sequence of events in a story or selection and knows the importance of each event as a part of a larger story or account.

Since functional, or work-type, skills are necessary for finding important information for a report or other types of assignments, the reader should develop the following competencies:

1. Uses table of contents of a volume in a proper manner.
2. Employs different dictionaries and glossaries for finding various word meanings.
3. Utilizes such specialized sources as the *World Almanac, Read-*

er's Guide to Periodical Literature, and various encyclopedias for finding specific pieces of information.

4. Demonstrates that his skimming techniques are adequate for discovering if a given volume or article contains desired facts.

Since every child should develop a genuine love for reading, the following characteristics should be evident in the growth pattern of every reader:

1. Enjoys reading as a free-time activity.
2. Reads many different kinds of books in a variety of subject areas.
3. Shares stories with his teacher and other pupils.
4. Evidences pleasure in "selling" a book or selection to another child.
5. Implements information gained from wide reading into content area assignments.

Obviously, many of the previous goals will not be reached by every slow-learning child. The important factors of level of intelligence, motivation, physical health, and mental health should be significant considerations in determining the degree to which any child can accomplish these objectives. A careful evaluation should be conducted at various stages during the child's educational training to discover which goals have been reached, how they can be obtained, and a determination of the objectives that will probably never be reached.

BUILDING AN EFFECTIVE READING PROGRAM

Reading programs which meet the needs of the slow-learning children require careful investigation and thought. Both long-range and short-term goals must be established, along with the formation and application of materials and techniques which will help the teacher to achieve these goals. The following principles may well be the key towards building such a program. Successful, optimistic, innovative teachers use these principles to accomplish maximum reading gain for their pupils.

1. *Reading assignments must be approached through a planned sequence if they are to be meaningful.* In the *first* place, appropriate readiness for the reading assignment must be made. An investiga-

tion on the part of both teachers and pupils should be conducted to note the nature of the topic to be read. The chapter headings and the subtopics should be observed in order for the pupil to get a feeling for the subject. If the topic under consideration is "the Amazon jungle," the teacher might ask questions such as these: "Have any of you ever visited the Amazon area?" "Do you suppose the farmers of that area grow wheat and corn, or do you think they grow other crops?" "Look at the picture on page sixty-seven. Do you think you would like to live in this part of the world?" "How far away is the Amazon jungle area from our city?" "Do you suppose the people of that area eat the same kinds of foods as we do?"

In addition to the questioning technique, some teachers have employed media devices such as films, filmstrips, records, and tapes for building overall interest and readiness. In still other cases, the use of a resource person might be advisable. Stimulating and eye-catching bulletin boards which have been arranged by pupils can often be effective in building interest.

A part of the readiness stage is that of the introduction of new words and their meanings. New words and phrases should be used in sentences (never in lists) to show pupils the correct meaning of the various words. Review and introduction of word-analysis skill techniques should be used at this point. Phonetic and structural analysis generalizations should be emphasized in an inductive manner. Pupils who have particular difficulty with these concepts should receive special remedial help by the classroom teacher or the reading specialist at a later time.

The importance of the readiness stage cannot be underestimated. Unless the child (and particularly the slow learner) has adequate motivation for wanting to read, the efforts of the teacher will be in vain. Far too many instructors merely assign pupils to "read Chapter 3 and we'll discuss it," and as a result, the total learning experience is disappointing for both the child and teacher.

The *second* stage of an effective reading lesson is the formation of guiding questions which will serve as purposes for reading. The origin of these questions should come from at least three sources: the teacher, the pupils, and the author of the text(s). In a given situation, the teacher may say to the pupils: "As you read the next section, keep these two questions in mind: What was the real cause for the outbreak of disease among the pioneers? How did Lewis and Clark solve the problem of carrying supplies to the Northwest Territory?" She should elicit questions from the students after they have had a chance to skim the titles of the various headings and subheadings. (Even though a question which cannot be answered by the material in a text is submitted by a child, the query should be written down so students will be motivated to look in several sources for information.) Most writers include questions at the close of chapters or sections of many texts. A selected few of these should be used, since they supposedly correlate with the written material. With respect to the total body of guiding questions, the majority of the items should be those composed by the students. Unless the learner is made a direct part of the reading process, very little interest is generated for reading even small amounts of printed matter.

The *third* stage of the procedure is that of careful reading of selected sources to find the answers to the guiding questions. Since there is a wide span of reading levels present among any group of slow-learning pupils, the teacher must provide for a large number of source books which have a high level of interest and are written on many different reading levels. Each student needs to read from a book which represents his instructional level (at least 95% oral reading accuracy and 75% silent reading comprehension). To help a child to find books on his instructional level, the "five-finger" approach may be useful. In using this method, the child is told to count 100 words in the book he wishes to read. He is then asked to spread the fingers of one hand in an outstretched manner and each time he finds a word he cannot pronounce he bends one finger towards the palm of his hand. If he bends all five fingers down before he has read the 100-word selection, he is to assume that the book is too difficult and he should find an easier source. The writers have noticed many teachers of problem learners use this system with much enthusiasm and success. The entire process builds independence on the part of the child and helps him to form realistic judgments regarding appropriate reading materials.

There are many publishing companies which are marketing materials in the content areas for disabled readers. Many of these materials are described in the appendices of this volume. Teachers who have limited budgets for such aids can often find parallel sources in public libraries.

The *final* step of the reading procedure should be that of discussing the answers to the questions which were formed in the second step. Effective silent and oral re-reading skills can be taught and reviewed. If two pupils, for example, disagree with respect to an answer given to a question, the teacher might say, "Harold, would you read the paragraph aloud which proves that you are right?" If the entire class failed to find the answer to a given question, the teacher might say, "The answer to question number three is found on page sixty-five. Would each of you re-read that page silently and raise your hand when you have found the answer?"

A number of culminating activities such as painting of murals, making broomstick movies, writing stories and plays, and constructing dioramas might be quite useful and interesting. Some teachers have used the videotape camera to good advantage in constructing movies, class documentaries, and scenes from plays.

2. *Effective planning for reading instruction can only come about when a very thorough analysis has been made of each pupil's reading strengths and limitations.* A pupil's competency (or lack of it) is a sum total of many parts. In some cases, he may have class-level skills in word analysis, below-level achievement in some or all of the comprehension areas, but very adequate understandings with regard to functional reading abilities. It is not enough to merely say that a child is a "poor" reader. Several techniques and instruments must be used to evaluate every major phase of the reading skills area.

The use of a reading survey test (such as the *Nelson Silent Reading Test, Botel Reading Inventory,* or the *California Phonics Survey*) as early as the second week of the school year would be very advisable. Class record sheets would indicate the nature of possible instructional groups which should be formed, along with hints relating to the possible goals which should be stressed during the semester. These tests also reveal grade-placement scores; however, the teacher should keep in mind that these scores tend to be frustration statistics, and the true instructional level of a given child is probably one or more grades lower than the test score indicates. With the slow learner, the element of "guessing" may be significant and should definitely be taken into consideration by the teacher.

Individual diagnostic instruments may be more useful for slow-learning children than any other tool. The *Diagnostic Reading Scales* and the *Durrell Analysis of Reading Difficulty* are two of the most common tests used for diagnostic purposes. These tests should be given by the reading specialist; however, innovative classroom teachers can give them after they have had sufficient practice and study.

The use of teacher-made informal tests to discover items relating to a given child's interests, critical reading ability, and word-attack skills can be of great value. Descriptions of some of these tests are included in Chapter IV.

Despite the effectiveness of both commercial and informal tests, they must be supplemented by the astute observation of the teacher. Such aspects as reading attitudes and frustrations surrounding the reading act cannot be measured by any man-made test. The amount of information which can be derived from informal interviews between child and teacher must be an integral part of any evaluation program.

After a designated body of data has been collected for each child, the teacher should ask herself the following questions:

a. In light of this information, what kinds of materials should I use with this child if he is to achieve maximum growth in reading skills?

b. What is his potential reading level when his general intelligence is considered?

c. What kinds of word-attack skills cause him the most difficulty?

d. Does our room and school library contain books which are on his instructional and interest levels? If not, where can I get them?

e. Considering his pattern of oral reading, do I need to establish individual help sessions to aid him in removing such errors as omissions, substitutions, and refusals?

f. Which area(s) of comprehension need the most reinforcement and/or reteaching?

    g. Do I need to refer the child to the school psychologist, nurse, or reading specialist for a further diagnosis of his reading difficulties?

    h. Can I best serve his needs by placing him in a small reading group, working with him individually, or having him attend special reading class?

    3. *There is no one reading approach or method which is far superior to all other procedures in meeting the reading needs of retarded learners.* The advertisements in professional journals would lead a teacher to think that a given product is a cure-all for all reading problems of both normal and slow-learning pupils. Some persons sincerely believe that "Brand X" is the absolute answer to many reading problems. The results of the recent national first-grade studies which were sponsored by the United States Office of Education indicated very clearly that no one approach was so much better than all other methods. One must keep in mind that teacher competency is a much more important ingredient in a successful reading program than any given set of reading materials. A well-qualified teacher must have materials, however, if she is to do an outstanding job. One must complement the other.

    To get some idea of the effectiveness of given materials when used with a certain group of pupils, the teacher should use sample sets of aids as a pilot project to determine pupil acceptance or rejection of a given technique. Since building reading skills is a highly individualized matter, the teacher must always look upon herself as a reading "pharmacist" and select parts of many aids to fit the needs of a given child. Children have many different learning modalities, and the use of any single "canned" system can hardly be justified in view of the many proven facts about the learning rates of humans.

    At the present time, a few companies have signed "performance" contracts with school systems and if their products do not create desired reading growth, the company cannot collect the money for the aids. Some of the companies have allegedly removed slow learners and those with IQ's below a certain level from contract considerations. Teachers of slow-learning children would do well to investigate all phases of such contracts before becoming a party to any agreement.

    4. *Reading instruction should be oriented to preventing serious*

reading problems instead of trying to remediate them after they have become serious. As a director of a university reading clinic for a number of years, I am sincerely convinced that trying to overcome long-standing reading difficulties of pupils who are 10 to 11 years old or older is a complex assignment. For example, the senior-high boy who has an instructional reading level equal to most sixth-grade children presents a very challenging situation.

Teachers must practice preventive reading in the same manner in which doctors practice preventive medicine. Children can most certainly be identified at a very early age with respect to learning and reading-retardation symptoms. Large amounts of money should be spent for organizing programs at the primary-grade levels to help these children. In some cases, large groups of mothers in a community can be organized to help pupils. The *Volunteer Aids in Reading* is the name of a group of 700 mothers in the Omaha metropolitan area who have been helping primary children learn various reading skills under the direction of the classroom teacher. Special emphasis has been placed on helping the retarded learner because of the sizable time demands which the teacher encounters in trying to help these pupils. The mothers complete a special preservice institute which is conducted by the Central Reading Clinic, at which time they are taught how to help pupils with sight word skills, phonic generalizations, vocabulary-building exercises, and spelling exercises. At the time this paragraph was written, the available evidence pointed to the fact that these pupils are being aided immensely by the procedures in the primary grades, and the amount of remedial help necessary at the intermediate and upper-grade levels has been greatly reduced.

A number of commercial tests are now available for helping school officials identify the child who is destined to have learning difficulties. Some authorities[2,3] mention one or more of the following tests for this purpose: *Frostig Test of Visual Perception* (Follett), the *Beery-Buktenica Developmental Test of Visual-Motor Integration* (Follett), the *McGahan Early Detection Inventory* (Follett), the *Screening Tests for Identifying Children with Specific Language Disability* (Educators Publishing Service), *First Grade Screening Test* (American Guidance), *Illinois Tests of Psycholinguistic Abilities* (University of Illinois Press), and *Psychoedu-*

cational Profile of Basic Learning Abilities (Consulting Psychologists Press). When a number of these tests is used and the results placed in an overall profile, much valuable information can be obtained which will be of great help to the primary teacher in overcoming basic learning problems. The preventive instructional program which is devised for a given child (especially the slow learner) should be a joint effort of the classroom teacher, school psychologist, reading specialist, and other school officials.

5. *The end product of any reading program should be geared to building a love for reading on the part of every child.* Teachers should provide a learning atmosphere which results in a genuine desire for reading as a leisure-time activity and not because a certain number of pages have been assigned as a required lesson. Boys and girls should have a chance to read from a large number of books in many subject areas and on many ability levels. When Hazel or Sam says, "I sure like this book," or "Do we have to stop reading now?" the teacher will know that she has "arrived" with regard to that child.

There are a number of ways available to the teacher to promote free reading. One of the most popular methods is that of using paperback books which are available in large quantities from many companies and are quite inexpensive. Commercial book clubs are being used in some systems to promote leisure-time reading. Brief oral book reviews and the use of pupil-made bulletin boards are also ways of stimulating wide reading activities.

6. *Reading activities which employ the use of oral reading skills should be an important part of any reading program for the slow-learning child.* Careful provision must be made for using oral reading activities in a developmental-reading program. Most children find that reading aloud is a pleasurable activity which gives them a feeling that they have really participated in a reading lesson. Oral reading can also serve as a meaningful diagnostic tool for the teacher in discovering a given child's word-analysis errors. In using oral reading activities, there are a number of principles which every teacher should keep in mind.

In the first place, a child should always read a selection silently before reading it aloud (unless the teacher is using it for diagnostic purposes). He needs to get acquainted with the subject matter of the text, the type of phrasing involved, and the nature of the diffi-cult words which he has perhaps never encountered before.

Secondly, an audience situation must prevail when oral reading is undertaken. There is no place in a well-devised reading lesson for "round robin" reading which calls for one child to follow another in reading a given selection. In this environment, there is no real purpose for reading, members of the audience become bored if the reader is having pronunciation difficulties, and the insecure child is under a certain amount of tension if he knows he will be unable to unlock certain words which appear in his section.

Third, the teacher should seize meaningful opportunities which will develop and extend oral reading skills. Some of these activities might be as follows[1]:

 a. Reading orally a story or play for entertainment purposes.

 b. Reading the minutes of the last club meeting in order to in-form the members of the actions which have been taken in the past.

 c. Reading aloud a statement from a textbook or other source to substantiate or refute a remark made by the speaker or an-other classmate regarding a particular subject.

 d. Reading aloud an important announcement which is of im-portance to all members of the audience.

 e. Reading orally to others a particular part in a play which the class has composed.

 f. Reading aloud to provide information which will help to solve a question which has arisen during a social studies or science lesson.

 g. Reading orally a limerick in order to demonstrate rhythm in verse.

 h. Reading aloud with the use of the tape recorder in order to listen to the actual mistakes made by the reader and thus serve to call attention to those oral reading areas which need fur-ther strengthening.

 i. Reading a story or poem aloud in unison with a number of other pupils, which serves to develop self-confidence and poise in an audience situation.

 j. Reading a short story or poem to illustrate a lesson or moral.

 7. *Developing an effective reading rate for each child should be*

an important goal of every teacher. Many pupils develop an undesirable habit of reading all materials at the same speed, regardless of
the difficulty of reading matter. Among slow learners, the problem
of hesitant, repetitive reading appears to be widespread. In many
cases, they are plagued by basic word analysis problems, which in
turn creates word-by-word reading associated with subvocalization,
finger-pointing, and other unsatisfactory tendencies. The teacher's
chief objective should be that of getting the pupil to be a versatile
reader—that is, he can read at a slow, meticulous rate when reading
for details; at a moderate rate when looking for a main idea; and at
a skimming rate when trying to find a single detail or fact.

The first step in helping a child with reading-rate problems is
that of trying to discover the causes for the problem. Does the child
lack basic word-attack skills for unlocking words? Is he fully motivated for the reading task? Does he understand that rate depends on
the reader's purpose? These questions must be answered before
significant progress can be made with respect to helping the child in
this area. One important item must be kept in mind by both pupil
and teacher: *a pupil cannot read any faster than he can comprehend
the material which is being read.*

There are several ways of helping a child improve his rate of
reading. In order to give the pupil the proper motivation for reading, a distinct purpose must be given for the reading assignment.
The teacher might say, "Read carefully the first two paragraphs on
page forty-six and tell me what three materials are needed to make
the corner shelf."

The use of the tape recorder can be effective in relating to the
child how he reads. He can play the tape and then listen to a recording which has been read at the proper rate of speed. If there is
good rapport between the teacher and pupil, this activity can be
most useful.

A few children are aided through the use of mechanical pacing
devices. If they are not hampered by serious word-attack problems,
these aids may help them double their reading speed without loss
of comprehension.

8. *Each teacher should help each child develop a high level of
listening skills.* One of the distracting factors for a number of children in learning to read successfully is the basic inability to listen

to oral directions, factual presentations, and even fictional material. These same children have difficulty in hearing likenesses and differences in sounds and cannot associate the verbal with the written symbol of words. The slow learner is typically quite retarded in listening growth.

There are a number of techniques which the teacher can employ to aid listening skills. First, the pupil must understand the purpose of listening. He must know, for example, that the ability to listen carefully might be critical in the case of impending disaster such as when the teacher says, "There is a fire in the east hallway. Follow me immediately out of the west exit!" In another situation, the teacher might explain to the pupils that the directions for the assignment will be given only once and those who fail to listen will need to remain after the dismissal bell has sounded to have them repeated. (The previous suggestion is practical if the children are without organic hearing difficulties and the chief problem appears to be careless listening habits.)

Secondly, the length of time which is used for a listening activity must be carefully assessed for the slow-learning child, since his attention span may be relatively short. Listening activities which call for close attention on the part of the pupils should be planned for the part of the day when the vast majority of the students are rested, alert, and ready for such activity. As a practical matter, one might find that reading a chapter from an interesting book for sheer pleasure immediately following the recess period is much more desirable than an activity which demands that the children remember every detail of an announcement, for example.

Finally, the teacher must remember that the physical aspects of the room must be taken into consideration in planning listening activities. To insure maximum success, she should be sure that the chairs are comfortable, the temperature is at an adequate level, and the lighting is proper. Doors should be closed to eliminate as many distracting noises as possible.

There are a number of other items which one might include as guideposts in building an effective reading program; however, the preceding items appear to constitute the major facets of any successful reading effort.

THE RELATIONSHIP OF WORD ANALYSIS, COMPREHENSION, ORAL READING, AND STUDY SKILLS TO THE TOTAL READING ACT

As indicated in an earlier section, there are a large number of components involved in the total act of reading. Each is dependent on the other for complete mastery of gaining meaning from the printed page. The items included in the above heading are dealt with in a detailed fashion in later chapters; therefore, a brief discussion of the interrelationship of these facets is sufficient at this point.

The first major step in derivation of meaning is that of *word analysis.* The slow learner must understand the importance of using phonetic and structural analysis skills (as well as other techniques) in the process of unlocking words. While some meaning is possible without literally pronouncing each and every word, he must understand that his level of understanding is reduced in proportion to the number of words not mastered. Word analysis is the center, or heart, of the reading process, and most research studies of the causes of deficient reading seem to indicate that this factor is one of the most important items which has been delineated by researchers. Lack of word-attack skills is by far the most common difficulty of problem readers. Formal and informal devices which might be used for the evaluation of word analysis are described in Chapter IV.

Comprehension is the end product of reading and is probably the most important facet of the reading process. As the child grows older, he commonly does much more silent than oral reading and is asked to respond to oral and written questions from his teacher regarding the facts, principles, and ideas which have been presented in a given article or chapter.

One must understand that *comprehension* consists of much more than just reading for details or getting the main idea. Also involved in this process are such items as reading to generalize; reading maps, graphs, and charts; differentiating between facts and opinions; understanding the writer's intent; obtaining an impression of the writer's style; and following directions. Some of these aspects are primary, or lower, comprehension skills which are developed at the lower elementary levels, while other facets (such as understanding the writer's intent) are introduced and taught at the middle and upper-grade levels as well as in the high school.

Oral reading is important in any ongoing developmental reading program; however, it is probably one of the most misunderstood reading concepts among teachers of average and slow-learning children. When oral reading is properly employed in a reading program, it can be used as an important evaluative device and can serve as a tool for reading enjoyment for many pupils. In such cases, an audience situation must always prevail and the reader must always have a distinct reason for the oral reading. In far too many cases, children are asked in "round-robin" fashion to read a common selection, and boredom is the inevitable result for many of the readers. Teachers must remember that slow learners must never read orally from a book which is above their instructional reading level. Independent-level books are actually preferred for such assignments, since these pupils need immediate success and have short-term goals.

One of the most difficult skills to develop with slow learners (as well as other children) is that of *study skills.* Proficiency in this area calls for the reader to make numerous decisions such as which book to use, where to find the book, and how to use the volume. Reading in specialized sources for maximum understanding depends on adequate word-analysis and comprehension skills. Evaluative procedures which are described later in this volume should be used to determine each child's competency in this important area. Areas of deficiency should be remediated through the use of specialized teaching techniques to insure meaning from content-area materials.

SUMMARY

In summary, every teacher should be acquainted with the reading goals for the slow learner and build those skills which are needed by individual children. Reading assignments which are approached through a four-step sequence will help to achieve this purpose.

Careful evaluation of each pupil's ability and the selection of the proper approach and materials for use with the child in overcoming his reading limitations are important considerations. Preventing reading problems before they have a chance to develop should be an important objective of each instructor. The final test of any reading instructional program is the degree to which each child loves to read and treats books as his friends.

One must keep in mind that there are several significant facets to the total reading act and all of these are related. Teaching priorities should be geared to the respective facets according to their importance to the total reading act, as described in the latter portion of this chapter.

REFERENCES

1. Cushenbery, Donald C.: *Reading Improvement in the Elementary School.* West Nyack, Parker, 1969, p. 50. Reprinted by permission.
2. Bond, Guy L. and Tinker, Miles A.: *Reading Difficulties: Their Diagnosis and Correction.* New York, Appleton, 1967.
3. Harris, Albert J.: *How To Increase Reading Ability,* 5th ed. New York, McKay, 1970.

Chapter III

PROMOTING READING READINESS FOR THE SLOW LEARNER

KENNETH J. GILREATH

The role of reading readiness and its place in the total reading picture is not merely that of a preliminary activity to the total program. It is more than simply that which comes first. It is rather the brick, mortar, and sand of which the firm foundation of the entire reading program is based. The readiness program for the slow learner must go beyond the stage of simply preparing the child for success in reading. It must also anticipate and aid in solving the various learning problems which plague the child in his academic endeavors.

MENTAL AGE AND READINESS

A great deal of research and educational thinking has concerned itself with the problem of when a child should begin reading, and the often-suggested figure of 6 years, 6 months is not a universally accepted one.

The initial study in this area was published by Morphett and Washburne[1] in 1931. A number of first-grade children were tested to measure their intelligence at the beginning of the year and then given reading achievement tests in February. Seventy-eight per cent of the group who had a measured mental age of 6.5 (6 years, 6 months) made satisfactory growth in reading, while those under that figure showed proportionately less than satisfactory growth. Gates[2] and others have questioned the contention that a critical point exists on the mental-age scale, pointing out that other factors exist which also affect the time which is "right" for learning to read. Perhaps I should say that while the best evidence available does not prescribe an exact mental age for beginning reading, the data does indicate the importance of mental age along with such other factors as effective curriculum, teaching methods, and teachers.

The teacher of the slow learner is faced with an even more critical problem relative to the proper time to begin reading activities. Because the child may be slower in his mental activity or possess other handicaps which retard his achievement, the mental age becomes an important factor. The knowledge that a child functions at a 6-year–6-month level will be of more value than an IQ score of 75 or a chronological age of 8 years, 6 months. The awareness that many children are not ready to begin reading at the same time as their peers and the patience to "wait them out" are valuable abilities for a teacher to possess. Readiness activities and materials designed to meet the interest levels of these children, as well as to overcome their specific learning disabilities, will go far in insuring ultimate success in reading.

A general guide for the teacher to assist her in judging the child's mental maturity might be as follows.

1. *Understands Directions.* If the child is able to understand directions, follow directions and perhaps even give directions to others, he has a "leg up" on the process of reading. A further development in the process of handling directions would deal with the concept of following directions within the area of group distractability.

2. *Reading Interest and Attention Span.* Perhaps one of the most often repeated concepts related to the slow learner is that he has a short attention span. The questionable aspect of this is that we also observe many of these children totally absorbed in activities for long periods of time. The child who spends hours listening to a phonograph record or being totally absorbed in a television commercial would indicate that with proper motivation and adequate development of interest, even slow learners can acquire the type of attention necessary for reading.

3. *Development of Memory.* One of the major learning problems of the slow learner lies in the area of memory. The several studies which have been done in this area show that overlearning procedures can compensate for this weakness.

4. *Desire and Need for Reading.* A desire to read and an interest in reading material are generally all that is necessary for motivating

the normal child. The slow learner, however, often must be put in a situation in which he has a strong *need* for reading. This is particularly true of the child who has spent several fruitless years in school and has not developed reading skills. A part-time job that is enjoyed by the student or an opportunity for job advancement, have proven to be very effective in providing the necessary push for achieving success in reading.

5. *Development of a Good Self-Concept.* The acquisition of a good and objective self-concept cannot be overemphasized. It is readily apparent that when readiness does not come at the regular time, it can easily be replaced with feelings of inadequacy and failure. The child who is realistic about his weaknesses as well as optimistic about his assets and abilities will be able to deal effectively with his failures. He will be able to approach the additional problems of readiness in a manner designed to succeed.

EXPERIMENTAL BACKGROUND

In this country, the family plays a vital role in the early development of a child's potential. The development of physical, social, intellectual, and emotional potential during the early formative years rests exclusively with the home and family. The cultural deprivation that occurs within the family structure of our nation's poverty-stricken people reflects a major problem relative to readiness for reading.

Some of the more serious problems resulting from poverty and the associated deprivations might be as follows:

1. *The Working Mother.* The mother-child relationship is a vital one. All too often, poverty-area mothers are forced to work because the father cannot provide adequately for the needs of the family or because it is easier and more profitable for the mother to find employment. The children are left in charge of older siblings or are left to fend for themselves. The pressures of life in this country's poverty pockets also tend to destroy the mother-child relationship. The combination of too many children, too little time, and too little room creates an atmosphere that inhibits or retards the development of academic potential.

2. *The Matriarchal Family.* The early breaking-up of slave families, along with some of the conditions of our welfare programs,

have produced the matriarchal family within our society. The results of this are detrimental, particularly to male children. The female-dominated households, often with a grandmother or an aunt in addition to the mother, are sometimes set in an atmosphere of illegitimacy, desertion, law violation, and imprisonment. The females in the home often have a poor attitude toward males. This leaves the male child without an adequate male model. The popularity of street gangs is partially the result of these youngsters' search for a masculine image. These young men also display total rejection to anything suggestive of femininity. Because of the high incidence of women in the school setting, these boys equate it to femininity also, thus beginning school with an attitude of belligerence. The lack of motivation often is present before the child even begins school.

3. *Verbal Ability.* Language development and its effect on the slow learner relative to reading readiness will be discussed later in this chapter; however, in poverty areas some unique language problems exist. Because of crowded conditions, noise pollution is a constant problem (neighbors, their televisions and radios, etc.) ; thus any additional noise, such as children verbalizing, is discouraged by the parent. The parents themselves are often deficient in language ability, thereby depriving the children of an adequate language model. An additional barrier to language development of the poor child is the scarcity of objects in the home. Children better associate linguistic meaning to objects which they have encountered. Perhaps the most serious verbal liability of the poverty child lies in the area of sound discrimination. Hurley[3] points out that the constant din within the home and neighborhood is uncomfortable to the infant, thus causing him to deaden his mind to the stimulus of sound. This *teaches* the child to be inattentive. He does not learn to discriminate between sounds or to distinguish important sounds (teacher directions) from unimportant sounds (traffic on the street outside the school room) .

These are but a few of the problems which face a poverty child as he enters school. The suggested solutions for these problems have ranged from educational reform to social reform, and there is reason to believe that gross changes in both areas will be necessary to eliminate the problems of the poor. The most immediate need certainly lies with the school, and preparing these children to succeed in reading should have first priority.

PHYSICAL FACTORS IN READINESS

A child's readiness to read also depends on his physical readiness. The sensory capacities of vision and hearing, as well as such factors as speech and health are recognized as vital to success in reading.

Vision

Visual problems are often the cause of a child's experiencing difficulty in learning to read. While it is true that many children with poor vision ultimately become excellent readers, it is equally true that poor vision very often creates problems in learning to read effectively. The teacher should therefore be on the alert for behavior patterns on the part of the children which would indicate a need for an eye examination. Some of these behavior characteristics are as follows:

1. Excessive brushing or rubbing of eyes.
2. Closing one eye, frowning, tilting of the head.
3. Stumbling or tripping over small objects.
4. Holding books or objects too close to his eyes.
5. Strabismus (crossed or walleyedness), dizziness.
6. Complaints of headaches when doing close work.
7. Inflamed, red-rimmed, or watery eyes.

If the child demonstrates any of the above characteristics, a visual examination should be made.

Another very common visual problem found among young children is hyperopia (farsightedness). A child with this problem may see quite well and even pass a Snellen test (this is the test used by school nurses and many physicians for pre-school examinations). He may be able to read material on the chalkboard, but he is still ill-equipped to handle material 12 to 14 inches from his eyes.

It is important to realize, therefore, that the child who displays behavior characteristic of a person with vision problems will need an eye examination that includes the far-vision tests as well as tests for near vision and binocular vision.

Visual Discrimination

Visual discrimination is described as those visual skills necessary for children to learn to recognize words. Many children, particularly those who fall into the slow-learner category, experience a great deal of difficulty in this area. Fortunately, instruction in visual perception has proven to be successful. Instruction has been proven effective in teaching children to see likenesses and differences in geometric figures, pictures, letters, and words. The lessons should range from the very obvious differences and likenesses to those which are progressively more subtle. The many commercially prepared materials which are available are very effective and are usually sufficient to meet the needs of most students. Teacher-made materials are often helpful if used on an individual basis to meet the specific needs of individual students.

Word discrimination is often developed further by utilization of the immediate surroundings. Calling attention to the likenesses and differences of words and letters in signs, on chalkboards and bulletin boards, and in stories the teacher reads is an effective motivation for learning to discriminate visually.

Hearing

Helen Keller and others afflicted with the dual handicap of blindness and deafness tell us that the greater handicap of the two is that of deafness. The educational implication of this information should be that we emphasize the auditory area of teaching even more than we do. The ability to discriminate sounds auditorily is certainly an advantage in speech and probably gives an important boost to learning to read.

The problem of sound discrimination that afflicts the culturally disadvantaged has been previously discussed, and the discrimination problems of the bilingual child are also great. These problems are, however, above and beyond the auditory problems of most slow learners.

These children typically experience problems of discriminating between whole words such as "bat" and "sat." It has also been shown that even when children can identify the differences in the beginning sounds and the total conformation of word sounds as in the example above, they often fail in transferring this knowledge to different positions, as exemplified in the word "*A t*lantic."

Another problem area for many children is the inability to discriminate speech sounds. Robinson[4] points out that reading success is linked with this skill in two ways: its relation to language and speech and its role in phonic analysis. The general problem here is not in the child's inability to hear the speech sounds but in his ability to discriminate between the fine differences in the sounds.

Successful reading also depends on efficiency in auditory memory. Slow-learning children exhibit problems in this area by displaying several areas of forgetfulness. They forget directions given to them, they forget stories read to them, and they forget or confuse similar statements and/or words. Training designed to improve a child's auditory memory can be achieved through devices designed to aid the child in locating sound and remembering where it came from. Tape recordings of various familiar and unfamiliar sounds and rhythm-band instruments also aid in developing auditory discrimination.

Sequencing of sounds is a valuable tool for a slow-learning child to acquire. Producing a variety of different sounds, either vocally or mechanically, and having the children attempt to reproduce them in the sequence they were given is often beneficial in developing auditory memory.

SPEECH DEVELOPMENT

Speech problems, particularly those relating to articulation disorders and delayed speech, are frequently mentioned as causative factors in reading difficulties. Because both of these functions are language related and therefore somewhat interdependent, a deficiency in one often leads to a deficiency in the other. Because speech evolves before reading, any problems apparent in this function would obviously affect the reading process. Whether these articulation and/or delayed speech problems result from sound-discrimination inadequacies, as has been mentioned earlier, from maturational delays, or from inadequacies in the child's experiencial background, the important fact to remember is that they do often impede reading and should be considered in diagnostic procedures.

LANGUAGE DEVELOPMENT

Perhaps more than any other concept, the concept of language development relates to all areas of maturation. The importance of experience, mental maturity, and visual, auditory, and speech development to the reading process has been discussed. The success of all children in achieving growth in each of these areas depends to a large extent upon their developing language skills.

The first aspect of language that is learned by a child is oral. He acquires the ability to make sounds and becomes pleased with the sounds he makes and with himself for making them. This success encourages him to put various sounds together. Loving parents then identify these sounds as meaningful words. At this stage, parents and others begin to reinforce his vocalization by applying (often with a great deal of imagination) meaning to his utterances. It is at this developmental point that the child begins to achieve meaningful language. How well this language develops and how efficiently the child utilizes it depends on many things, and slow learners, particularly, experience a number of difficulties.

Slow-learning preschool children often have a very limited communicative ability. The language at home (as in the case of the culturally disadvantaged) is often limited to commands which have the effect of limiting receptive language. "Shut up" does not require a discriminating listening situation, nor does it give an opportunity to make a linguistic response. The need exists in this situation for the child to develop elaborate language. If, for example, the mother would ask the child to "Be a little more quiet because Mother is talking on the phone," the child would be able to experience shades of difference in such areas as tone of voice and loudness. Hopefully he might also begin to see the relationship between acceptable behavior and praise from parents.

The language process is a most important one in all school curricula. It touches every goal and function of the school, and every child learns to use language skills in all of the following ways:

1. *Language and Socialization.* Before learning can take place in a classroom, the teacher must establish social control. This is best achieved through the medium of language.

2. *Language and Emotional Adjustment.* The use of language tells us much about the psychological needs of children. A child's

eagerness for ego-satisfaction is very often reflected in loud, abusive language. Another child might withdraw as a result of failure and cease using language completely, thus indicating by his language failure some emotional problems.

3. *Language and Mental Growth.* The total language level of retarded children is typically lower than their mental age. This fact lends credence to the statement that the development of language is vital to an individual's mental growth. Intelligence can be acceptably described as the ability to do abstract thinking. One of the better examples of abstract thinking is the process of manipulating the symbolic materials of language in a meaningful fashion.

It is obvious that because language does play such a vital part in the development of all the prereading factors, it must be considered very carefully by the teacher of slow-learning children. The whole reading-readiness process is dependent upon a sound language background.

ASSESSMENT OF READING READINESS

The evaluation of reading readiness for slow learners differs from that for the normal student in that careful consideration must be given to the amount of developmental retardation that exists within the individual. In some cases, it might be necessary to consider whether or not the child has a potential for reading; and in all cases it is vital that an accurate evaluation of mental age be achieved. It is recommended that some acceptable standardized intelligence-test form be administered.

The revised edition of the *Stanford-Binet* is often used and is generally considered to provide satisfactory estimates of a child's potential. The test is highly verbal and relies rather heavily on language development and experiential background. *The Wechsler Intelligence Scale for Children* (WISC) is also often used and has the advantage of utilizing both verbal and nonverbal performances. The evaluation of slow learners is aided by tapping both of these areas. Both the *Stanford-Binet* and the *Wechsler* are individual tests and require administration by a qualified and skilled psychometrist.

The *Illinois Test of Psycholinguistic Abilities* (ITPA) is valuable in assessing reading readiness of slow learners. It evaluates various language factors, such as visual and auditory memory and association, vocal and motoric expression, and understanding of what is seen and heard. Because slow-learning children are often language delayed, the diagnostic assistance of this test is most beneficial.

When evaluating prereading readiness of slow learners, it is also important to consider the need to place these children in educational situations where they can experience success. The adjustment of the children, both socially and emotionally, is most important. The teacher will want to evaluate their ability to succeed in situations which resemble reading before involving the child in a program.

Also available to the teacher of slow-learning children are the standardized instruments designed to measure the child's ability to profit from instruction in reading. A number of these tests are available and several of them can be administered by teachers. Rather than discussing these tests individually, it would seem advisable to comment on their purpose and those areas of readiness skills which are evaluated.

The reading-readiness tests serve the purpose of measuring several of the skills related to beginning reading. They are generally administered as group tests, but may include subtests which must be given individually. The tests of reading readiness measure such areas as picture directions, word matching, rhyming, and letter and number recognition. Other abilities tested by the readiness tests include auditory and visual discrimination, and learning rate.

DEVELOPING READING READINESS

In preparing and selecting materials for assisting the slow learner in reading readiness, it is important to remember the following:

1. The slow learner will need more opportunities for repetitive trials. Materials should be designed to allow for more trials than are needed for normal children.
2. Materials should be highly motivational. Because so many slow learners are not eager students, the materials used should be selected for their appeal to the student. Colorful games, charts, puzzles, and concrete objects are effective in meeting this need.
3. Materials should be designed for success. The slow-learning

child must not be overchallenged; he will progress if the materials and activities are within his capability.

With these few basic rules in mind, the teacher can proceed in her search for effective reading-readiness materials.

Suggested Activities and Techniques

The following list of suggested activities and techniques will serve as a guide in the selection of materials.

DIRECTION GAME. The object of this game is to develop within the child an ability to listen, and to develop memory span as well as the ability to follow directions. Cut-out objects such as cars, houses, or dogs contain a series of directions on the reverse side. The child selects an object and the teacher reads the directions to the child. The sequence may contain one, two, or more directions as follows:

1. Take three giant steps forward, turn around two times, walk slowly back to your seat.
2. Walk quietly to the teacher's desk, knock five times, hop back to your seat.
3. Touch your head and then your toes, count to three and tickle your nose.
4. Walk over to a friend, shake hands with him, tell him your name and your address.

There are, of course, many different activities of this kind that you may use, and it is quite easy to keep the rest of the class interested and involved by having them check to see that each student is following the directions correctly.

DIRECTION BOX. This is another activity that is effective in developing attention span and the ability to follow directions. Each child is given three small boxes which are numbered and a selection of different-colored poker chips. The oral directions are graduated in difficulty from such instructions as "Put two red chips in box one" to more complicated efforts such as "Put one red chip from box one into box three." The degree of difficulty can be increased as the children grow in ability.

Developing a Longer Attention Span

The attention span of slow learners often is short, and teachers will want to create activities designed to develop the child's ability to attend for longer periods of time. These activities should be highly motivational and relate directly to the child's area of interest. The following ideas should prove helpful in this area.

WHAT IS MISSING? Find pictures of familiar objects such as cars, horses, television sets, or pets. Cut out the pictures in such a way that an important part of the object is missing. Have the children identify the missing part. The teacher might also wish to discuss the importance of the missing part to the rest of the object. This activity can be varied in a number of ways. A part of the several pictures can be cut out and children can then match the missing part with the right picture. Pictures can also be designed with something wrong, such as a fish in a bird's nest or a dog with a cat's head. The children are asked to find what is wrong with the picture. There are several good commercially prepared materials that follow this same theme and they can be purchased in most teacher supply stores.

LIFE-SIZE SELF-PORTRAIT. One of the more exciting activities for the young slow learner is that of making a life-size picture of himself. The children lie on a piece of butcher paper and the teacher traces around them. The students then add the detail, carefully observing the color of hair, eyes, and clothing. The portraits are then labeled and displayed. This also makes an attractive method of identifying a child's desk for such events as open house or parent conferences.

Convincing the Child That He Can Read

The slow learner is usually involved in reading-readiness programs for much longer periods of time than are normal children. This means that his chronological peer group will be reading long before he is ready to do so. The result of this lag is often frustration and defeat on the part of the slow learner. This frustration manifests itself in such a way that it is necessary to develop a quite different type of prereading program. One of the more effective techniques to use with the older prereader is to convince him that he can indeed read.

PICTURE DICTIONARY. The teacher and the student sit together and page through a popular magazine to identify words that the child can sight read. He will be surprised to discover that he recognizes a number of words, such as "Coca Cola," "Winston," "Ford," "beans," and many others. His success in this activity will motivate him to continue on his own. The procedure is as follows:

1. The student cuts out pictures of familiar objects, pastes them on sheets of notebook paper, and with the teacher's help labels them.
2. The teacher then prints the word in a sentence that the child has dictated.
3. The pictures are arranged in alphabetical order and secured in a notebook.
4. The child practices reading the word and the sentence. (This would include practice with the picture covered.)

This activity is not only highly motivational but also a great help in building the child's self-concept.

EXPERIENCE CHARTS. The development of an experience chart is initiated by the teacher beginning a discussion dealing with any current interesting event. It can deal with holidays, movies, field trips, television programs, or any item that interests the children. The class then dictates a story resulting from the discussion and the teacher prints it on the chalkboard. The story should be kept very short and very simple and should include many repetitions. The story can then be copied by the children, either on the board or on ditto copies. Sequencing can be taught by putting the words on cards and mixing them up. Additional interest can be given to the experience chart by utilizing a camera (Polaroid is best) and adding pictures.

Increasing Visual Perception

Materials to help increase visual perception can be developed by the teacher, or they can be found in commercially prepared packages. (Those prepared by Marianne Frostig[5] are recommended.) The materials are designed to identify problems in several areas and to provide remedial activities in those areas where help is needed. The program deals with five areas of visual perception. They are as follows:

1. Eye-hand coordination, which requires that the student draw left to right lines between two boundaries of different width and shape.
2. Figure ground exercise which involves being able to select an

object hidden against backgrounds of increasing complexity.

3. Constancy-of-shape test, which requires an ability to discriminate among different shapes such as circles, squares, and ellipses of varied size, textures, and positions.
4. Position in space, which presents familiar objects in reversals and rotations for identification.
5. Spatial-relationship activity, which requires the child to analyze form and pattern relative to lines and angles.

This program provides an excellent diagnostic tool as well as effective training in perceptual skills.

Increasing Sound Discrimination and Auditory Memory

The problems of sound discrimination and auditory memory are such that they lend themselves effectively to game activities. The teacher can design activities which are enjoyable as well as developmental.

WHO AM I TALKING ABOUT? The teacher tells the children to close their eyes and listen. Then she says, "I'm telling about a boy who has on a blue shirt and brown shoes. He has light hair. Open your eyes and signal when you know." Variation of this game would be to have them keep their eyes closed and tell who it is.

DRAW WHAT YOU SEE. The teacher tells a story. For example: "I saw a pretty house. It was white. The roof was green, the door was brown, the chimney was red. Draw and color the pretty house."

DO WHAT I DO. The teacher taps out a pattern with her pencil and chooses a child to repeat the same pattern: 1. tap, tap, rest, tap. 2. very quick taps, five in a row.

These kinds of activities are effective as fillers before and after lunch breaks or recess.

Correcting Speech Problems

Speech problems of the slow learner are best dealt with by a qualified speech correctionist. There are, however, many opportunities for the classroom teacher to assist these children. There are many games and activities which lend themselves well to assisting children with delayed speech.

WHAT'S IN THE BAG? A cloth laundry bag is filled with a variety of familiar objects. The child who is "it" reaches into the bag and selects one of the objects. Then, without naming the object, he describes it in such a manner as to allow the class to guess what it is. The child who guesses the object is allowed to describe the next object.

THE ECHO GAME. The teacher sets the stage by pronouncing correctly the various problem words in the form of a poem or verse. The children repeat after her. Example:

> What does a bird do?
> Fly, Fly, Fly.
> What does a baby do?
> Cry, Cry, Cry.
> What does a snake do?
> Hiss, Hiss, Hiss.
> What does a mama do?
> Kiss, Kiss, Kiss.

Creative use of such objects as the telephone and tape recorder are also valuable in improving speech in slow learners, as are activities such as role-playing, telling stories, show-and-tell (bring-and-brag), riddles, and finger plays.

Language skills for the slow learner should, of course, be included in all of the child's prereading activities. In addition, the teacher will want to devise activities that encourage students to practice using complete sentences and more elaborate language.

SUMMARY

In summary, reading readiness for the slow learner must concern itself not only with many of the same problems as those faced by normal children but also with those problems that are related to the child's learning difficulties. Many of these children need additional assistance from the teacher in the areas of developing mental maturity and improving experiential background. The physical characteristics of vision and hearing are also necessary to reading and are often underdeveloped in the slow learner. Speech and language development are closely related to the reading process. Because language is so closely associated with all of the readiness functions, it must receive special attention.

After it has been determined through acceptable evaluative procedures that the slow-learning child has reached a developmental level that will make reading-readiness instruction worthwhile, the teacher should select and develop materials designed to meet the student's special needs. These materials must be highly motivational and should be presented on a level that will insure success.

REFERENCES

1. Morphett, Mabel V. and Washburne, Carleton: When should children begin to read? *Elementary School Journal, 31*:496–503, 1931.
2. Gates, A.I: The necessary mental age for beginning reading. *Elementary School Journal, 37*:497–508, 1937.
3. Hurley, Roger: *Poverty and Mental Retardation, A Causal Relationship.* New York, Random House, 1969, pp. 78–79.
4. Robinson, Helen: Factors which influence success in reading. *Elementary School Journal, 55*:263–269, 1955.
5. Frostig, Marianne *et al.*: *Manual for the Marianne Frostig Tests of Visual Perception.* Palo Alto, California, Consulting Psychologists Press, 1966.

Chapter IV

EVALUATING READING COMPETENCY

Donald C. Cushenbery

In most school systems, educators construct curriculum guides which outline the scope and sequence of the reading skills which should be mastered by all children in the district. Because pupils have widely varying learning styles and levels of motivation, some of them (especially slow learners) are unable to reach these goals. In order to assess their present abilities in each of the predetermined skill areas, a number of diagnostic procedures should be undertaken. The data from these techniques and procedures should be used to plan effective instructional programs to help pupils strengthen their limitations in reading. The sections which follow contain a discussion of the kinds of diagnostic instruments available for evaluating reading skills, along with information relating to the proper use of the data obtained from the tools.

REASONS FOR EVALUATION

The use of evaluative procedures has four major functions. First of all, information can be gained regarding which instructional goals have been met. For example, if a second-grade teacher has the objective of teaching three new vowel digraphs to a group of slow-learning children, she can decide if her goal has been met by administering a commercial or informal word-analysis test of the kinds mentioned later in this chapter. The future instructional goals of the teacher should be altered according to the results of the evaluative instrument.

Secondly, testing and careful observation of slow-learning children is important for the purpose of aiding teachers in finding the most appropriate materials and techniques for use with individual pupils. The results obtained from the *Wepman Auditory Discrim-*

ination Test, for example, may indicate that the best procedure for a certain child would be a strong aural approach. In other cases, the test data might suggest the use of a tactile approach, such as the Fernald technique.

Another major purpose of evaluation is that of determining the reading competencies of all pupils in reading-skill areas. Information from these instruments can lend data relative to the major strengths and limitations of an entire school population. Careful study of the results can help to pinpoint those students who have difficulty in certain areas and who need specific remedial lessons to help them overcome their deficiencies.

A fourth reason for conducting a program of reading analysis is for the purpose of grouping pupils who have similar instructional needs. The total curriculum can thus be explored with greater facility on the part of the teacher.

KINDS OF EVALUATIVE INSTRUMENTS

Nearly all evaluative tools can be grouped into various categories: commercial and informal, individual and group, and survey and diagnostic. There are several questions which a teacher should answer before test choices are made. Some of these are:

1. What reading skills do I want to evaluate?
2. How much time do I have available for the procedures?
3. Is the validity and reliability of the test (s) at a high level?
4. Have other local educators found the instruments useful for evaluative purposes?
5. Is the test format and type size suitable for the pupils who will be using the instrument?
6. Are monies available in the school budget for ordering the necessary tests?
7. Can the instrument be machine scored as well as hand scored?
8. Are the test results easy to interpret?
9. What comments are made about the test in *Reading Tests and Reviews* (Gryphon Press) ?
10. Does the test have alternate forms?

DESCRIPTIONS OF COMMERCIAL TESTS AVAILABLE FOR MEASURING READING AND RELATED SKILLS OF SLOW LEARNERS

There are a large number of reading and psychological instruments which are available for use by the classroom teacher, school psychologist, and educational specialist. Reading-survey tests are normally used on a classwide or schoolwide basis to measure general reading achievement and to detect those pupils who may need intensive remedial help. Individual diagnostic tests should be administered to students who have complex learning-reading problems. Psychological tests of the variety noted in the next section can be employed by psychologists and other related specialists to add further diagnostic data in order that a more meaningful reading program can be established for given pupils.

The tests listed below may be used with slow learners and comprise a small number of the total instruments available in each category. The reader may wish to consult volumes by Harris[1] and Bond and Tinker[2] for further information.

Group Survey Reading Tests

Botel Reading Inventory (Follett) is designed for grades 1 through 12 and supplies information relating to reading instructional level. It includes subtests dealing with the general area of word recognition and phonics in a specific sense.

Comprehensive Tests of Basic Skills (California Test Bureau) comprises four levels of tests for grades 1 through 12 and contains sections dealing with reading vocabulary and comprehension.

Gates-MacGinitie Reading Tests (Teachers College Press) has five levels of tests for grades 1 through 12 and measures such items as vocabulary, comprehension, and speed and accuracy.

Nelson Silent Reading Test (Houghton-Mifflin) is designed for grades 3 through 9 and measures vocabulary and paragraph comprehension.

S.R.A. Reading Record (Science Research Associates) should be employed with high school students to analyze such items as comprehension; rate; paragraph meaning; reading of directions, indexes, and advertisements; and general vocabulary.

Individual Diagnostic Reading Tests

Durrell Analysis of Reading Difficulty: New Edition (Harcourt, Brace, Jovanovich) consists of several subtests for elementary pupils which are designed to evaluate listening comprehension, silent reading, oral reading, and general word analysis including phonics, writing, and spelling.

Gates-McKillop Reading Diagnostic Tests (Teachers College Press) are especially suitable for slow learners and retarded readers and consist of two forms for evaluating word analysis, comprehension, syllabication, letter names and sounds, and visual and auditory blending.

Gilmore Oral Reading Test, New Edition (Harcourt, Brace, Jovanovich) may be employed with elementary-school students for measuring oral reading accuracy, rate, and comprehension.

Gray Oral Reading Test (Bobbs-Merrill) may be used in grades 1 through 10 for evaluating oral reading errors (which lend help in diagnosing oral reading problems) and general comprehension ability.

Diagnostic Reading Scales (California Test Bureau) is suitable for all grade levels and lends valuable data relating to abilities in vocabulary, sight words, comprehension, phonics, and instructional reading levels.

Psychological Instruments

Analysis of Learning Potential (Harcourt, Brace, Jovanovich) consists of five different test levels for the assessment of school learning ability for pupils in grades 1 through 12. The subtests emphasize word-relational concepts, number concepts, and figure concepts.

Chicago Non-Verbal Examination (Psychological Corporation) can be administered to all school age groups for gathering intelligence data. The instrument is nonverbal and requires no reading; thus it is especially useful with subjects with limited intelligence.

D.A.T. Verbal Reasoning, Numerical Ability, and Abstract Reasoning Tests (Psychological Corporation) require little reading and are designed for high-school students for gaining data relating to general intelligence and scholastic aptitude.

Detroit Beginning First-Grade Intelligence Test, Revised (Harcourt, Brace, Jovanovich) requires no reading and can be used in group situations.

First Grade Screening Test (American Guidance) is designed to analyze potential learning disability, emotional and social adjustment, and general perceptual and intellectual capabilities.

Illinois Tests of Psycholinguistic Abilities (University of Illinois Press) can be employed with preschool through fourth-grade students to determine strengths and limitations in basic communication skill areas.

Kindergarten Evaluation of Learning Potential: KELP (California Test Bureau) evaluates basic learning components of young children and provides insights to the examiner relative to the basic readiness skills of pupils.

Minnesota Percepto-Diagnostic Test (Clinical Psychology Publishing) lends information relative to possible neurological irregularities of children and adults.

Oseretsky Motor Proficiency Tests (American Guidance) measures the ability of elementary- and high-school students to perform body motor tasks.

Purdue Perceptual-Motor Survey (Charles E. Merrill Books) analyzes the basic areas of motor and visual control as well as laterality and left-to-right orientation. The instrument is designed principally for use with primary-school children.

Screening Test for the Assignment of Remedial Treatments (Priority Innovations) may be used in group situations with preschool and first-grade children for measuring ability in visual copying and discrimination in addition to visual and auditory memory.

Wepman Auditory Discrimination Test (Language Research Associates) evaluates the primary-school child's competency in distinguishing the differences in sounds in pairs of spoken words. (Since auditory discrimination is a significant factor in learning to read, this aspect should be studied for every slow-learning child.)

THE CONSTRUCTION AND USE OF TEACHER-MADE READING TESTS

The use of informal or teacher-made instruments for supplying information relative to a given child's present reading skill development should be considered important. Few commercial standardized tests can measure with complete accuracy the scope and sequence of a given local school reading program. Teachers can build and adapt various kinds of informal tests for measuring such abilities as word-recognition skills, general level of comprehension, oral reading, the intent of an author, reading interests, scanning and skimming, sight word vocabulary, and instructional reading level.

Two questions should be answered by every classroom teacher of the slow learning child: How does his reading potential (or capacity) reading level compare with his actual instructional level? To what degree do the books and materials meet the actual reading needs of individual pupils in the classroom? The answers to these two questions can rarely be obtained from the usual commercial instruments. I have successfully used the techniques described in the following sections for obtaining this type of information.

Techniques for Finding Reading-Potential Level

The teacher must understand that the reading-potential level is that level where the child should function in terms of the number of years he has been in school as calculated from his present mental ability as assessed by a reputable, trained examiner. The mental age and/or intelligence quotient should be obtained from an individual measure whenever possible for the greatest amount of accuracy.

According to Bond and Tinker,[3] reading expectancy can be obtained through the use of the following formula:

$$\text{Reading Expectancy} = (\text{Years in School} \times \frac{\text{IQ}}{100}) + 1$$

For example, if Sam, a third-grade pupil, is evaluated in the month of January, has an IQ of 80, and has never been retained, his reading expectancy would be

$$(2.5 \times \frac{80}{100}) + 1 = 3.0.$$

In the above case, Sam's reading expectancy is 3.0, although the grade level for his class is 3.5; therefore, if he is reading at or above 3.0, he is performing at the *expected* level. Some teachers and other specialists espouse the principle of "bringing everyone up to grade level"; however, this goal is virtually impossible to attain in the cases of pupils with deficient mental-age levels when this formula is applied. There are some pupils who can *never* be brought up to grade level, and this fact should be realized by persons working with slow-learning children.

Reading-expectancy scores should be figured for all pupils in a given classroom to determine which students are disabled readers (those reading *below* expected levels). As a general rule, those boys and girls who exhibit actual instructional levels which are two or more grade levels below potential level, should be given intensive remedial work to help them reach their potential level. This goal is possible if there are no severe emotional or physical problems present to complicate the remediation process. In case these problems are in evidence, a multiprofessional approach should be undertaken with the classroom teacher, psychologist, and the medical specialist working together to achieve the highest reading level possible under the circumstances which are present.

The formula described earlier places a high premium on the use of intelligence test scores; therefore the selection of tests is an important item. Many reading specialists prefer to use the information obtained from individual measures such as the *Stanford-Binet*, the *Wechsler Intelligence Scale for Children*, or the *Peabody Picture Vocabulary Test*. Information obtained from intelligence instruments which yield verbal and nonverbal data (such as the *Lorge-Thorndike Intelligence Test*) may be especially helpful for use with those subjects who have severe reading difficulties. Tests which place much major emphasis on verbal aspects should be avoided, since the instruments would have a tendency to evaluate reading skills instead of basic mental abilities.

Measuring the Instructional Reading Level

The materials and techniques which are used in the reading curriculum for the slow-learning child should always be geared to his *instructional* level. Briefly stated, this is the level where he can read the material from a given level with 95 per cent accuracy when reading *aloud*. Silent reading comprehension must be at least 75 per cent on both literal and inferential-type questions.

One of the best ways of measuring the instructional reading level is through the use of an informal reading inventory. The instrument is not difficult to make, and the information derived from the procedures is invaluable in constructing a suitable learning program. Far too many children are being forced to read from frustration level (that level where a subject scores less than 95 per cent oral reading accuracy and less than 75 per cent silent reading comprehension), and as a result, the child becomes discouraged and may eventually become a school dropout if easier material is not used.

The following steps should be used in constructing the informal reading inventory:

1. Locate a series of basal readers which contain stories of approximate equal interest for boys and girls. The books should not be familiar to the pupils who are to use the inventory; therefore, a set of supplementary basal materials would probably be most applicable. A typical story of from six to eight pages from each grade-level book should be selected for use. If possible, the various pages of the stories should be cut from the book with a razor blade and placed between clear acetate sheets for use in a notebook. (If stories cannot be cut out of the books, bookmarks can be placed at the story locations, and the various volumes can be used for the different selections.) Each story should be separated with a stiff piece of paper such as a piece of file folder. Tabs can be constructed at the side of the notebook so one can turn to a given story with ease.

2. For each story, make a red line at a point approximately three-fourths through the selection. This mark designates the place where the pupil should stop his silent reading and where he starts the oral reading.

3. For a given subject, turn to a selection which represents the approximate instructional reading level of the child. Mention something of interest about the selection in order to establish readiness for the reading act. Say to the child, "Will you please read silently to this red mark on page forty-five? When you reach this point, tell me and I will ask you some questions about the story you have read."

4. A series of comprehension questions involving such comprehension skills strands as reading for details, main ideas, differentiating between fact and opinion, and general organization should be constructed for each of the stories. A given number of possible

points should be allowed for each item (usually between 5–15). The section below illustrates how one might organize such a test.

	Possible Points	Pupil's Points
Comprehension of Silent Reading		

Main idea.

What were three things the cats did to tease Bill?
(The cats tipped the pot of soup, hid the spoon, and pulled strings out of John's pillows.) — 15 _____

Noting details.

a. Where did the boys find the two small cats? (They found them in a garage.) — 5 _____

b. Where did the cats sleep in John's home? (The cats slept on an old cotton coat under a log. If not clear, say "can you tell me more?") — 10 _____

c. What did John feed the cats when they were tiny? (He fed them warm milk.) — 5 _____

Inferred meaning.

a. Why did John finally chase the cats out of the house? (Because the cats got into too much mischief in the house.) — 10 _____

b. What did the cats do when something outdoors frightened them? (They ran into the house and crawled under their bench. If not clear, say "Can you tell me more?") — 10 _____

Organization.

a. What did the cats do the first few weeks in the house? (They just drank milk and slept. They didn't move away from their bed.) — 10 _____

b. What did John finally wish he could do with the cats? (He wished he could sell them to the neighbors.) — 10 _____

Vocabulary (5 points each).

a. furry
b. waddling
c. instantly
d. unsafe
e. noticed — 25 _____

Total Comprehension — 100 _____

Comprehension Standard: Independent level = 90–100 per cent.
Instructional level = 75–89 per cent.
Frustration level = 74–0 per cent.

In applying the comprehension standard, the teacher should go to the next lower level story if the comprehension score is considerably less than 94 per cent; if the score is 98 per cent or above, the next higher level should be employed.

5. After the comprehension questions have been asked, the subject should be asked to read the remainder of the story orally. A copy of the story should be typed double-spaced and used with a clipboard. While the child reads aloud, appropriate symbols should be employed to denote oral reading errors. The following designations are used by some reading specialists for this purpose: *omissions*, circle word left out; *substitutions*, draw a line through printed word and write substituted word above; *insertions*, use inverted "V" mark in the sentence where word was inserted and then write the word that was said; *refusals*, underline word refused; *repetitions*, one wavy line under word for each repetition.

At the conclusion of the oral reading exercises, calculate the oral reading accuracy by dividing the total number of words included in the selection into the total number of words pronounced correctly. For example, if a 500-word exercise was employed and the subject made 20 oral reading errors, the oral reading score would be 96 per cent (480 divided by 500). The *oral reading standard* with respect to reading levels is as follows:

    a. Independent level, 98 to 100 per cent.

    b. Instructional level, 95 to 97 per cent.

    c. Frustration level, 94 per cent or less.

6. If there is a gross discrepancy between the comprehension and oral reading accuracy scores in attempting to compute a given reading level, the comprehension score should take precedence, since the end product of reading is getting meaning from the printed page. One may have a subject who makes a score of 93 per cent on silent reading comprehension and 90 per cent in oral reading. A given subject may have a comprehension score in the independent range and an oral reading figure at the frustration level. The comprehension score should denote the level of books and materials to be used by the student; however, a more careful study should be made of the child to see if he has certain word analysis errors.

Checking the Suitability of a Textbook

In working with the slow learner, the selection of suitable reading materials is a crucial item. While the use of an individual reading inventory (such as the one described in the previous section) is preferred for finding the exact reading level of a given student, there are group procedures which one might use to achieve the same purpose. We have used the following technique with much success with slow-learning children. You may want to adapt it slightly for your situation.

1. Select a series of content books which may be close to the instructional reading levels of the majority of the students who will be using the materials.
2. Locate approximately two pages of nonfictional material which contain some specific facts of a detailed nature. Compile 10 comprehension-type questions of both factual and inferential items which are taken from the pages in question.
3. Ask all students in a given group to read the material silently and to close their books once they have completed the reading. Admonish them to wait quietly until all have finished the task.
4. Give each student a copy of the test and ask him to supply the correct answers. The examination should be carefully scored with 10 percentage points allotted for each question. One may assume tentatively that all students who score at or above 70 per cent can "handle" the text; those with 50 to 70 per cent scores have questionable abilities; and pupils who have less than 50 per cent must be given easier material to read.

Assessing Sight Vocabulary Ability

Since word analysis is the heart of the reading act, the assessment of each pupil's sight word vocabulary is important. Many years ago, a leading reading authority, Dr. Edward Dolch, devised the Dolch Basic Sight Word List which constitutes a significant percentage of the words found in the primary levels of most basal reader series. While the *Dolch Basic Sight Word Test* (Garrard Press) can be used for evaluating sight word competency, there are informal devices which may be used. The following is a word-practice sentence test * which makes use of a large number of the Dolch words. (Any

---

* This test is printed by permission of Omaha Public Schools system.

child who has at least a third grade reading level should be able to read the sentences with ease. If he cannot, the remediation techniques described in Chapter V should be undertaken.)

1. May is a month away.
2. Does he know how to do it this way?
3. She is a kind lady.
4. This is a real fine house you have.
5. Can you find ten black cats?
6. These are both of the twins.
7. Sit anywhere in the room over there.
8. There is always a name for everything.
9. Why didn't you laugh at the clown?
10. He was not funny.
11. How did he do it?
12. We are going to hunt birds.
13. These are the ten apples.
14. Did she want the dress?
15. What did she say?
16. I went to the store.
17. Your eggs are getting warm.
18. I'm too full to eat lunch.
19. I own that house.
20. We should wash the car.
21. Many of them are small.
22. Your books are over there.
23. We are going to take a ride.
24. Must you go?
25. I am going to look upon you.
26. Some are small.
27. Get on the chair.
28. They came to play.

Evaluating Reading Interests and Attitudes

To meet the reading needs of any student, each teacher must not only know his potential and instructional reading levels but should also understand the nature of his reading interests and attitudes as well. This type of data cannot be derived satisfactorily from commercial instruments; therefore subjective or informal devices must be used. The following instrument[4] is a sample of one such tool.

1. Name_____ Age_____ Grade_____
2. From what source do you secure most of your free reading books?
   Friends_____ School Library_____ Community_____
   Library_____ Church Library_____
3. How many books have you borrowed during the past month?_____
   How many of the books did you read completely?_____
   Give the titles of some of the books. _____
   _____
4. Check the kinds of books which you like to read.
   Fiction_____ Mysteries_____ Sports_____
   Romance_____ Heroes_____ History_____ Science_____
5. What kinds of hobbies do you have? _____
   _____
6. List the names of three television programs you like best. _____
   _____
7. Give a list of the states and countries which you have visited. _____
   _____
8. Mention the names of three of your favorite newspapers. _____
   _____
9. Which of the following sections of the newspaper do you usually read?
   a. National and local news_____   d. Editorials_____
   b. Comics_____   e. Sports_____
   c. Feature stories_____   f. Other_____

Observing Reading Abilities in the Classroom

One of the most overlooked evaluation techniques with respect to reading is that of careful observation on the part of the classroom teacher. The technique of observation is a basic one and does not involve money for materials and techniques which are common with commercial and informal tools. Rapid generalizations can be obtained in a short period of time, and when these are supplemented with data from other sources, the teacher can come to some valid conclusions regarding such matters as the types of materials to use and the length of time a procedure should be employed.

There are a number of principles which should be remembered with respect to the use of observation as an evaluative device:

1. The teacher should concentrate her attention on a few pupils each day and record her observations instead of trying to deal with a large number of students.

2. For complete and adequate reading evaluation, the results obtained from this technique must be supplemented with data obtained from other sources.
3. The observer must have a broad background of understanding with respect to the forces acting on a child before he attempts to make valid generalizations with regard to behavior in a reading setting.
4. The "global" approach should be undertaken with each child. No firm conclusions should be drawn regarding a given child's reading competencies until a sizable number of observations have been made when a pupil is engaged in a common reading task such as oral reading, reading for meaning, or decoding a word.
5. A definite checklist of items should be kept in mind when making observations. The record indicated in the next selection may be used for this purpose. The exact items may need to be altered to conform to the objectives and standards which a teacher may have for a particular group of slow learners. The information should prove valuable in planning their instructional programs. Deficient items should be checked.

Pupil's name_____ Date_____

Vocabulary
Adequate_____

Language Development
Short, simple sentences_____
Below potential_____
Satisfactory level_____
Needs enlarging_____
Above expected level_____
Excessive word repetition_____

Speech Patterns
Distinct speech_____

Emotional Factors and Reading
Nervous and anxious_____
Volume too high_____
Confident and assured_____
Volume too soft_____
Rejects reading_____
Monotonous sound_____
Relaxed and enjoys
    reading_____
Stuttering present_____
Defensive about
    reading ability_____

Word-Analysis–Skill Development
Below expectation in
  terms of potential_____
Reverses words_____
Above expectation in
  terms of potential_____
Makes meaningful
  substitutions_____

Gross lack of phonics training_____

Guesses and unsure of most words_____

Substitutes words and phrases_____

Makes meaningless substitutions_____

Needs complete re-training in word analysis skills_____

Comprehension

Displays above average skill in all areas_____

Generally deficient in all areas_____

Locates significant details_____

Draws sensible conclusions_____

Differentiates between fact and opinion_____

Follows directions_____

Reads with little or no understanding_____

Gives ideas and facts not indicated in material read_____

Silent Reading Habits

Finds proper books for a specific purpose_____

Selects books at independent or instructional reading levels_____

Keeps at reading task and not easily distracted_____

Compiles notes from factual type material_____

Depends on teacher to find appropriate book_____

Displays lip and head movements_____

Distracted easily and not generally interested in reading assignment_____

Exhibits a narrow band of reading interests_____

As noted earlier, information derived from observation techniques must be obtained at different intervals and in various situations to secure valid conclusions regarding a given child's competency in reading. Those items which are consistently noted should receive the serious attention of the teacher. Reteaching techniques which are described in other parts of this volume should be used to overcome these deficiencies.

Assessing Reading Attitudes Through Informal Projective Techniques

Gaining valid information regarding a given child's reading attitudes can rarely be obtained through the use of commercial, standardized instruments. Because of this fact, the use of informal, teacher-administered, projective devices such as incomplete sentences or story telling represent an effective way of attaining attitudinal information. Teachers should refer those children who present severe attitude and/or emotional problems to the school psychologist or other specialist for an evaluation through the use of the *Thematic Apperception Test, Rorschach,* and similar instruments.

The following incomplete-sentence test has been used by the authors to obtain significant data relating to a given child's attitudes with respect to reading. The actual responses of a client have been included at the close of the test, along with the interpretation which might be given to the response patterns. (If the child cannot read the stimulus phrases, they should be read by the teacher and she should record his oral responses.)

Directions: Finish each of the following sentences with the word or words which tell exactly how you feel. Don't worry about getting anything wrong. Put down the first thing that comes to your mind. This is not a test and has nothing to do with your report-card grades.

1. I feel like _____
2. Sometimes I wish _____
3. I read when _____
4. If the teacher would _____
5. The books in this room _____
6. I am happy when _____
7. I wish my mother would _____
8. Reading stories is _____
9. When I am reading _____
10. I get mad when _____
11. My favorite subject is _____
12. I don't know why _____
13. Some days I would like to _____
14. The best part of the day is _____
15. School is _____
16. Most books are _____
17. I wish my report card _____
18. If I could read _____
19. My mother thinks I _____
20. I can read better than _____
21. If people would _____
22. No one likes _____
23. Homework is _____
24. I hope that _____
25. A good time is _____

Jerry Subject (not his real name), a client at the University of Nebraska at Omaha Reading Clinic, responded to a sampling of the above statements in the following manner:

1. I feel like telling the teacher that I don't want to read.
3. I read when the teacher makes me. But, I don't like to.
5. The books in this room look hard to me.
11. My favorite subject is math. Also, recess. That's when I can get out with the boys and play ball!
18. If I could read as well as my older brother, my Mom would be happy.
21. If people would help me, I could be a better reader.
24. I hope that I grow up to be rich.
25. A good time is out playin' games and not havin' to study.

The previous comments reveal much insight with respect to Jerry's attitude toward the total reading act. He sees reading as being extremely difficult and frustrating but thinks that he can improve to a limited degree if people would help him. There is also a suggestion that his difficulty with reading has caused parent rejection. This type of data is very helpful in developing a reteaching program for the child, since it appears that he not only needs skill reinforcement but psychological restructuring as well. Unless his attitude is made more positive toward reading, the prognosis for reading success will not be optimistic.

GUIDELINES FOR USING TEST DATA

The information obtained from both commercial and informal instruments can be very useful in planning developmental and remedial reading programs for the slow learner. In fact, unless careful evaluation procedures are undertaken, any program used with these children will tend to be a "hit-or-miss" affair and will have limited results. In order to make proper use of these tools, certain guidelines should be understood by the classroom teacher, administrator, and reading specialist.

1. *The results from a single test should never be considered final with respect to a given child's capabilities in reading.* The educator should always consider the total pattern of scores which come from a series of tests before making final conclusions regarding reading efficiency. There is always the possibility, for example, that a given child did not fully understand the directions for completing a comprehension section on one test, though his scores on all other

tests have been quite satisfactory for his age and grade. Sometimes pupils are temporarily upset or nervous on a given test on a particular day. In other instances, a very compulsive child might secure the correct answer to a number of questions on a test but fail to complete the total instrument in a given amount of time and thus receives a lower score than would normally be the case in a classroom reading situation.

2. *One should keep in mind that the reading grade placement score derived from many reading achievement tests tends to be a frustration score; thus the child's true instructional reading level may be a grade level or more below the test score figure.* Dr. Ned Marksheffel of Oregon State University comments that the records of students receiving help at his reading clinic during the period from 1958 to 1966 indicated that standardized tests of reading tended to place a student from one to four grade levels above his actual instructional reading level.[5]

The reason for the discrepancy factor is the result of the guessing element which is ever present in a test which is based on multiple-choice–type questions. A student may not really understand the basic meanings which should be derived from a given article, but because he has a good ability to choose logical answers, he may, in fact, score at an unrealistically high level.

3. *The process of evaluation should proceed on a continuous as well as a periodic basis.* Though careful planning is required for any well-devised reading program, actual lesson plans should be altered if and when the need arises. If, for example, the teacher notices that the particular series of phonics materials she is using is too complex for a given child, her careful observation should dictate the change to less difficult lessons. In some cases, results from periodic commercial tests indicate a long-term remedial prognosis for a given student; however, data from informal tools may indicate a more rapid improvement than was anticipated. Obviously, the teacher's goals should be revised in light of this condition.

4. *Careful attention should be given in choosing the proper instruments for measuring desired reading skills, habits, and attitudes.* All formal and informal tests have limited objectives with respect to reading assessment. Some, such as the *California Phonics Survey* measures the junior- and senior-high students' ability to apply cer-

tain phonic principles but does not purport to evaluate reading habits and/or attitudes. The sentence-completion test which was described earlier is designed to gain some impression regarding the child's attitude about reading but is of little or no help in analyzing his ability to read maps, graphs, and charts. The main principle to keep in mind with respect to total reading evaluation is to administer a general reading survey test (such as the *Nelson Reading Test* or *The California Reading Test*) to a total class or school and then follow it with a diagnostic test like the *Diagnostic Reading Scales* for those children who have a discrepancy of two years or more between the instructional reading level and the potential reading level.

SUMMARY

In summary, an alert teacher follows three sequential steps. He uses appropriate survey and diagnostic instruments for a complete evaluation of a child's reading strength and limitations; he builds an appropriate instructional program to satisfy the learner's needs; and he evaluates continuously to determine if the instructional procedures are meeting predetermined objectives.

REFERENCES

1. Harris, Albert J.: *How To Increase Reading Ability* (5th ed.). New York, McKay, 1970.
2. Bond, Guy L. and Tinker, Miles A.: *Reading Difficulties: Their Diagnosis and Correction.* New York, Appleton, 1967, Appendix.
3. *Ibid.,* pp. 92–93.
4. Cushenbery, Donald C.: *Reading Improvement in The Elementary School.* West Nyack, Parker, 1969, pp. 141–142. Reprinted by permission.
5. Marksheffel, Ned D.: *Better Reading in The Secondary School.* New York, Ronald, 1966, p. 87.

Chapter V

DEVELOPING WORD-ATTACK SKILLS

Donald C. Cushenbery

Since the heart of the reading act is that of decoding words, the best procedure for accomplishing this goal has long been a source of discussion among teachers and parents. With respect to this subject, Karlin[1] notes: "Word perception has been the subject of research, debate, study and speculation, and it is no small wonder that it continues to challenge the thoughtful efforts of reading educators, psychologists, linguists, and representatives of other disciplines to explain how it occurs."

For the past decade, we have carefully studied the causes of reading retardation. Though no one item can be delineated as being the one most important causal factor, the inability to unlock or decode words is certainly one of the most common items discovered. For some pupils, the cause of word-analysis weakness is the lack of training in phonics; for others, such aspects as frequent change of schools, auditory and visual deficiencies, and poor attitudes have all been responsible to varying degrees.

Building a suitable program of reading instruction which will insure that each child can analyze words is a challenging assignment. Finding the printed symbols which stand for a spoken sound is one of the most complex learning tasks for any child, especially the boy or girl who is in the slow-learning category. The mere fact that the English language is not a phonetically regular medium and contains a large number of silent letters is a major reason for a given child's problems in word-attack development. All pupils, regardless of ability, need to be exposed to a well-developed, sequential program of developmental reading lessons and activities which will help to insure success in this important area.

PRINCIPLES OF AN EFFECTIVE WORD ANALYSIS PROGRAM

To insure that slow-learning pupils receive maximum learning through a given school's word-skills curriculum, the following principles should be remembered.

1. *A scope and sequence chart should be constructed which outlines in sequential order the skills which need to be attained at different levels of the total educational program.* (Slow learners usually reach skill levels at a much later time than so-called normal children, and this aspect should be taken into consideration when assessing the progress of these pupils.)

2. *A careful diagnostic program which involves the use of commercial and informal instruments as well as teacher observation must be undertaken early in the school year to determine where each pupil is situated with respect to word skills development.* Using a pattern of scores from all of these devices and techniques, the teacher can establish a meaningful developmental and/or remedial program which is devised to meet his exact instructional needs.

3. *A number of decoding approaches should be considered, depending on the needs of particular children.* In some instances, a strong phonics program which is of a programmed nature may be the most effective. A more broadly based technique which employs structural analysis and context clues (in addition to phonetic analysis) may be the most practical. The aural approach which makes use of tapes, tape recorders, and headsets might well be the best procedure for some children. Each teacher should study diagnostic information, select the proper techniques in light of a child's learning pattern, and evaluate the learner's progress. If current teaching practices do not result in desired growth patterns, revisions in the instructional program should be made to accomplish this goal.

4. *The inductive, not the deductive, approach should be used in teaching phonetic and structural analysis principles.* Principles are more easily understood by the learner if they are able to "discover" them instead of having to learn them as "rules."

5. *Since most phonetic and structural analysis principles have a*

number of exceptions, they should be taught as generalizations and never as rules. A study by Clymer[2] indicated that some commonly taught phonic generalizations have a per cent of utility ranging from 0 to 100. He found, for example, that the common generalization, "when there are two vowels side by side, the long sound of the first one is heard and the second is usually silent," had only a 45 per cent utility.

6. *Differentiated instruction should be undertaken with word attack skill exercises assigned on a need basis.* Though a general, sequential program of overall skill development is both necessary and desirable, not all slow-learning pupils need identical assignments from a workbook or a series of exercises which have been prepared by the teacher. Training in phonics elements should always be a part of the regular reading lesson and never as an isolated activity. The pupils included in such classes should be assigned on the basis that they have demonstrated needs for such training. The range of pupil competencies in this and every other reading skill area will be broad ever for groups of slow learning children. Diagnostic evaluation instruments of both the commercial and teacher-made varieties which are described later in this chapter should be used to discover the true instructional needs of these pupils.

7. *Each child must understand that he should use a multiapproach to the task of decoding words.* As a general rule, he should learn to employ structural-analysis techniques first; phonic principles second; context clues third; and the dictionary fourth when he is trying to unlock a word. In any case, he should gain the understanding that he will probably use all of these approaches in the decoding process.

THE NATURE AND USE OF VARIOUS WORD-ATTACK TOOLS

As indicated earlier, any well-devised word-skills program consists of specific training in each of several decoding processes or tools. Since approximately 86 per cent of the words in our English language can, in fact, be unlocked through strictly phonetic techniques, the necessity for adequate and thorough instruction in phonics is all too clear. A sizable number of words contain prefixes, root words, and suffixes which lend themselves to structural analysis while other words must be seen in contextual situations before they can be decoded. (Examples of such words are "refuse" and "read.")

There are a few words which seemingly cannot be attacked by conventional generalizations which have been learned in typical reading programs. Graded dictionaries of the kinds mentioned in a later section of this chapter are a tremendous help to all children, particularly slow learners. There are certain principles which teachers should remember in helping pupils develop competencies in using this aid.

In order to give instructional insights into the nature and use of each of the four major word-attack tools, a discussion of these items is included in the next section. Appropriate teaching techniques for helping pupils develop appropriate skills in these areas are also included.

THE ROLE OF PHONICS IN THE WORD ANALYSIS PROGRAM

One of the most interesting aspects related to the history of educational programs in this country has been the periodic rise and fall of the importance of phonics training in reading programs. In order to secure a graphic view of the trends in this area, one should read of these accounts in any reputable history of education text such as *American Reading Instruction* by Nila B. Smith.[3]

There has been a raging controversy regarding the value of phonics since the beginning of private and public schools. In the late 1800's, the use of synthetic phonic programs which required each child to learn and recite long lists of word families was traditional and fashionable. Later, in the period beginning about 1925, a number of influential educators concluded that although many pupils could pronounce words with a high degree of accuracy, they could not attach meaning to the words in many cases. In light of this attitude, a downgrading of the importance of phonics was undertaken in the late 1920's and lasted until the late 1950's.

A number of books were written in the period from 1955 to 1965 regarding the alleged demise of phonics from popular reading programs, especially the basal reader systems. Rudolph Flesch's[4] *Why*

Johnny Can't Read caused intense emotional reaction on the part of both parents and teachers. In the late 1960's and early 1970's, intensive phonics systems were compiled and are now being used by many educators. Nearly every reputable reading program on the market today has a carefully balanced phonics training sequence as a part of the composite system.

Evaluation of Phonic Skills Abilities

In determining the kind and amount of phonics education which should be planned for the slow learner, a careful assessment of his present strengths and limitations in this area is vital and necessary. If this goal is accomplished, a number of principles should be remembered.

1. *Observe the child carefully when he is reading silently and orally.* When he reads silently, does he have a puzzled look on his face and display nervous tics and mannerisims which might be symptomatic of frustration in the process of decoding words? What oral reading errors does he make?

2. *Record and classify the kinds of oral reading errors a given child makes.* The teacher should have a copy of the reading material in her hands while the child reads aloud. The following procedures may be used to classify the errors:

   a. *Substitutions.* Cross out the printed word and write the word which was substituted above it.
   b. *Omissions.* Circle the word omitted.
   c. *Additions.* Place an inverted pointed symbol between the two words where the word was added. Write the additional word above the symbol.
   c. *Repetitions.* Draw one wavy line under the word which was repeated.
   e. *Refusals.* Put an "X" mark above the word refused.
   f. *Hesitations.* Place two "X" marks above a word if the child hesitated as long as four seconds before pronouncing it.

If this type of oral exercise is to have validity in the assessment of phonic abilities, the teacher should use a passage which contains a minimum of 100 words. An item analysis should be made of the six major error groups mentioned previously. The results of the analysis can help the teacher decide what kinds of phonic skills need remediation. For example, if a child says "cop" for "hop" and "mag" for "map" (and commits other similar errors), one might conclude that he needs help with both initial and final consonant sounds. Meaningless substitutions such as "house" for "horse" may indicate some knowledge of initial consonant sounds but a complete lack of understanding with regard to other phonic elements.

3. *Construct, administer, and analyze the results of an informal test relating to basic phonetic generalizations.* After having decided a given child's potential in reading, the teacher can determine the phonic principles that should be known by the child from the sequential list of skills mentioned later in this chapter. A convenient, informal procedure for completing this assignment is through the use of a subjective word-recognition skill test. The following items are samples of test items which might be constructed:

Initial Consonant Sounds. (Tell me what these groups of letters say.)

| pet | pem | for | fot | tar | taf |

Consonant Blends. (Pronounce these groups of letters for me.)

| shop | shoz | whet | whep | drum | drup |

Long and Short Vowel Sounds. (After I pronounce the word, tell me if the vowel has a long or short sound.)

| make | map | apple | hop | hope | use |

Hard and Soft Sounds of C and G. (Pronounce these words for me.)

| cit | calt | cel | gal | gof | gyp |

In each of the previous tests, a few nonsense words have been included along with familiar words. If a child truly understands the meaning and use of phonetic principles, he will be able to pronounce the nonsense words without difficulty. At least 10 items should be under each heading. If he scores less than 75 per cent on any one section, he may need remediation with respect to the principle in question.

4. *Commercial and basal reading series tests should be used to test specific phonic abilities.* The publishers of most basal reading programs and other series materials usually construct both placement and achievement tests for use by the teacher. There are other tests which are valuable and can be used with any reading program. Examples of such instruments would be the *Botel Reading Inventory* (Follett), *Doren Diagnostic Reading Test* (American Guidance

Services), and the *California Phonics Survey* (California Test Bureau). The first two tests listed are designed for primary and intermediate pupils, whereas the last test is for junior and senior-high students. Some individual reading tests such as the *Diagnostic Reading Scales* (California Test Bureau) and the *Durrell Analysis of Reading Ability* (Harcourt, Brace, Jovanovich) also contain phonic evaluation sections.

The Sequential Development of Phonic Abilities

If a teacher is to be of utmost help to the slow-learning child in phonic-skill growth, she must first of all find his reading instructional level and determine what can be realistically expected of him in terms of his mental age, years of school attendance, and other factors. After having determined this information, she then can gain an impression relative to the exact types of abilities which an individual child should possess. If she finds that a pupil should function at the fourth-grade level, then he should be able to exhibit satisfactory performance on all phonic elements which are normally introduced and taught at the first-, second-, and third-grade levels.

Though there are obviously slight discrepancies which might occur between scope and sequence charts which might be constructed by various reading authorities, the following chart[5] contains many of the common phonic elements which occur at the various grade levels.

1. *Readiness Level.* Readiness activities which stress auditory and visual discrimination: listening to sounds—high and low, soft and loud; listening to follow directions; telling a simple story in sequence; noting and reproducing sounds made by other children and the teacher; matching letters and words.

2. *Preprimer Level.* Reinforcement of readiness activities; developing a basic stock of 40 to 50 words; listening to and producing various initial consonant sounds; insight into the construction of simple compound words such as "play" and "ground" in the word "playgrounds"; noting words which rhyme; seeing the relationship between auditory and visual symbols with particular objects and pictures.

3. *Primer Level.* Attention to visual differences in words (con-

figuration); matching words and syllables with similar consonant sounds; recognizing various prefix and suffix forms such as "un," "non," "s," "ed," and "ing"; reciting and constructing short poems which have rhyming words; addition of 40 to 50 additional words to the basic stock of sight words.

4. *First-Grade Level.* Association of one consonant sound with double consonant letters at the end of a word (bell, toss) and with the two-letter symbols "wh," "th," and similar combinations; introduction of consonant blends ("tr," "gr," "gl," for example); substitution of consonant blends at the beginning of a word to form a new word in a story; knowledge of the concept of a root word as a meaning unit; attention to similar, but different words (were" and "wear," "then" and "when," for example).

5. *Second-Grade Level.* Review of the word-analysis procedures taught at the previous level; attacking new words by blending with initial consonants; developing consonant-sound relationships such as a consonant letter which represents more than one sound ("c" in "cost" and "cell"); two consonant letters may stand for one sound (the two "ll's" in "mill"); specific knowledge concerning long and short vowel sounds (the long "a" in "gate"; the short "a" in "apple"); identification and understanding of consonant digraphs ("ch," "sh," "th," "wh," for example); knowledge and use of open and closed syllables ("fo," "bo," "re," "pes," "rud," "sof," for example); understanding of the place of the final-"e" principle ("safe," "mite"); introduction of inflectional endings such as "es" and "est"; acquaintance with the principle of changing the final "y" to "i" in a word ("baby," "babies"); and recognition of words which are contractions.

6. *Third-Grade Level.* Applying word-analysis techniques to multisyllable words; study and employment of vowel digraphs, (such as *ea* in meat; *ai* in rain; *oa* in boat); diphthongs (*oi* in oil; *oy* in boy; *ou* in out, for example); and understanding of hard and soft sounds of "c" and "g"; study of the contractions and possessives that drop more than one letter; study of the alphabet preparatory to dictionary study; instruction in the application of the various syllabication principles; meaning of accents in syllables.

7. *Fourth-Grade Level.* Refining skill in the use of a number of word-perception skills in combination; review and necessary re-

teaching of skills introduced at the preceding levels; extensive use of the dictionary and all of its different parts; intensive study of synonyms, antonyms, and homonyms, and multiple word meanings; use of phonetic analysis in identifying words of three or more syllables; further introduction to prefixes and suffixes and their use as meaning units.

8. *Fifth- Through Twelfth-Grade Level.* Review and reteaching of any of the skills outlined at the lower grade levels; instruction in the area of structural analysis dealing with three or more syllable words; use of unabridged dictionary and other specialized aids; evaluating and planning each child's program in word recognition on the basis of individual need.

Classroom Activities for Building Phonic Skills

There are a large number of activities which make use of both commercial and teacher-made devices. Many of the commercial tools listed in the appendices of this volume may be used for developing and reinforcing abilities in the area of phonics. In most situations, companies which publish and produce such materials are willing to send descriptive literature with respect to the aids. The value of any given reading materials should be established in a pilot program setting before mass purchases are made.

There are many professional volumes which are available and relate to teacher-tested activities for aiding phonetic analysis skills. Some of these have been written by Dechant,[6] DeBoer and Dallman,[7] and Bond and Tinker.[8]

While older slow-learning pupils usually like the boxed materials and hardware media sets described in the appendices, younger boys and girls need intensive practice on phonetic principles in meaningful settings. Some of the most successful procedures we have employed during the past 25 years are included in the next section.

1. Phonic word wheels are always excellent interest arousers. The wheel can be constructed by making two circles from heavy posterboard. A large circle which is about eight inches in diameter and another one which is about five inches in diameter should be fastened together in the middle by a paper fastener, so that the smaller circle can move freely in a circle. Various word endings such as *one, ick, ip, op,* should be printed with a magic marker just

under the outer edge of the smaller circle. A rectangular slot should be cut on the outer edge of the smaller circle to expose the endings when the wheel is turned. Between the center fastener and the slot should be printed an appropriate consonant blend such as *st, gr, cr,* or *tr.* The child should spin the inner circle and pronounce the words. This technique can be used on a pupil-teacher or pupil-pupil basis with a high level of success.

2. Some pupils like to play phonic baseball. A baseball diamond should be drawn on a large sheet of heavy posterboard. Home plate and the various bases should be noted with round circles which are about two inches in diameter. Each child, using a round piece of colored posterboard (the same size as the bases), takes turn reading words which have been introduced in previous lessons. For each correct word a child reads while he is "at bat," he is allowed to move his circle to the next base. If he cannot pronounce the word, he loses his turn. The game can be played on an individual basis or groups of pupils can form teams.

A variation of the procedures for the phonic baseball game involves the "umpire" using a diamond which has been printed on an overhead transparency and projected on the screen. The movement of players around the diamond is fascinating when they see their progress through this medium.

3. Word checkers is easily played and enjoyed by nearly all young pupils. A regular inexpensive checkerboard can be used. The entire board should be laminated with clear film so it can be used repeatedly with different sets of words. A small felt-tipped magic marker which has yellow ink should be used for printing various words on the black squares. A player must take his turn, but he cannot move his checker to a desired location unless he can pronounce the word which occupies the space in question. Regular checker rules are used. After several pupils have played the game, words should be cleaned from the board and a new set of words used which the pupils have learned in past lessons.

4. A "call and mark" game can be used profitably to evaluate a pupil's ability to distinguish among various phonic sounds. Four lists of words (15 words in a list) should be typed (double-spaced) and duplicated for each of the pupils playing the game. Each pupil should be asked to follow directions such as the following:

a. Draw a circle around all of the words in the first list that have a short "a" sound.
b. Check the words in the second list that contain the hard "g" sound.
c. Underline the words in the third list that have a silent "e" in them.
d. Draw a line through all of the words in the last list that contain more than one syllable.

The directions and correct answers for this game can be recorded on tape by the teacher or one of the pupils in order that the activity can be self-corrective when used by a group of pupils who are equipped with headsets. When the answers are given on the tape, an explanation should be made regarding the reasoning for the response. In some cases, it may be desirable for certain pupils to repeat the exercise if they score below a certain predetermined level.

5. A circular word snail game is easily constructed and is enjoyed by most pupils when played by teams. A large snail-like pattern should be drawn on a piece of heavy white posterboard. The trail should be divided into 20 to 25 equal segments (the size of game cards described later), with the very innermost section designed the "home" segment. The child playing the game should have 20 to 25 numbered word cards (depending on the number of sections marked on the trail) which match the size of the trail segments. The cards are shuffled by a fellow student or the teacher, and if the child can pronounce a given word, the card is placed on the corresponding number section on the trail. Each pupil is given a single chance to pronounce a word. If he pronounces it correctly, it is placed on the proper space on the trail. Three or four persons can play the game, therefore each should have his own pattern card and word card set. The child who has the most cards on his trail at the end of the game is declared the winner.

THE IMPORTANCE OF STRUCTURAL ANALYSIS

A significant number of words in the English language contain two or more meaning units such as prefixes, root words, and suffixes. In the content areas of social studies, science, and mathematics, a pupil might discover as many as 20 to 30 multisyllabic words on a page which has been selected randomly. He might encounter the words "mismanagement" or "nonessential" as a part of his reading. If he understands the process for dividing such a word, he will find the prefixes "mis" and "non," proceed to attack the root words through phonic procedures, and pronounce the suffix "ment" through the application of the phonetic generalization which indicates that a medial vowel is generally short.

Compound words can be attacked through structural analysis when such words are regular in pronunciation. Examples of these words would be "grandfather" and "bookcase." There are a few words such as "breakfast" which are not regularly sounded in a compound situation and these exceptions need to be brought to the attention of the pupils.

Another type of structural analysis consists of the recognition and understanding of the inflectional endings of words. Visual scrutiny of words to note the common endings such as *s, es, ed, ing, er, est, t,* and *en* should begin as early as the first grade. Young children should know the singular and plural forms of words such as "book," "books"; "coat," "coats"; "elephant," "elephants"; and "lion," "lions."

There are a number of generalizations which should be remembered by the child if he is to gain a mastery of the total importance of structural analysis as a word-recognition tool. Dawson and Bamman[9] suggest the following list for this purpose:

1. Many inflectional variants are formed by adding endings with no change in the root word: walk*ing*, match*es*, call*ed*, girl*s*, go*ing*.

2. If the root word ends in the final *e*, the *e* is dropped when an ending that begins with a vowel is added: tak*ing*, bak*ed* (the *e* is dropped; *ed* is added), din*ing*. (An exception to this rule will be learned later: the *e* is retained on root words which end in *ce* and *ge*, if the ending which is added begins with an *a* or an *o*; examples: courage*ous*, trace*able*.)

3. If a monosyllable or root word ends in a single consonant, preceded by a vowel *(tip)*, the consonant may be doubled when an ending is added: tip*p*ed, swim*m*ing, fan*n*ed.

4. At the middle-grade level, the child will learn that the above

rule applies in polysyllables *only* if the root word is accented on the last syllable; for example: preferred', but pref'erence, ben'efited.

5. If the root word ends in *f*, the *f* is usually changed to a *v* before adding an ending: calves, knives, halves.

6. If the root word ends in *y* preceded by a consonant (*cry, deny*), the *y* is usually changed to an *i* before adding an ending: cried, cries; denied, denies. Note that this does not apply when adding -*ing*, since this would cause an awkward combination of two *i*'s: crying, denying.

7. If the final *y* is preceded by a vowel (*buy, monkey*), the ending is added with no change in the root word: buys, monkeys, played.

Suggestions for Developing Word Recognition Through Structural Analysis

The following are classroom-tested activities which can be used successfully with slow-learning children for the purpose of developing and reinforcing structural analysis skills.

1. A scrambled list of the first and second parts of regularly sounded compound words can be placed on one common list. Each word should be numbered and the child should see if he can find the two numbered words which go together to make a sensible word.

2. A list of ten common root words should be duplicated, along with a separate list of possible inflectional endings, prefixes, and suffixes. Each pupil should compose as many new words as possible by using the information found on the two sheets. Classroom dictionaries should be used by each person to check the accuracy of the list he has compiled. Recognition should be given to the individual who is able to compile the longest list.

3. An exciting syllable game consists of the flashing of words with one, two, and three syllables. Each child in the reading group has individual stacks of red, green, and yellow cards. When the teacher flashes a one-syllable word, the pupil is to hold up a red card; two-syllable word, a green card; and a three- or more-syllable word, a yellow card. This exercise serves both a developmental and remedial function. Pupils who have difficulty recognizing the number of

syllables should be given remedial training to correct the situation.

4. Lists of words which are known to the majority of the pupils could be noted on a sheet of paper. All words should contain one or more inflectional ends, prefixes, or suffixes. The boys and girls should be asked to draw a line under all parts of words that *are not* part of the root or base word.

5. To evaluate a pupil's understanding of prefixes and suffixes, compose a list of base words and ask him to make a new word which would change the spelling of the word and result in a new meaning for the word. For example the following items may be employed:

   a. What word is similar to "lawful" which means *not* lawful?

          _____lawful

   b. If I have more than one book, I would say

          I have many book_____.

   c. If I hit a ball yesterday, I would say

          I play_____ball yesterday.

6. The classroom or city newspaper can serve as an outstanding source of lessons for evaluating structural analysis skill abilities of slow learners. Select any three- or four-paragraph section of the paper which represents the instructional to independent reading level of most pupils and ask each of them to draw a line through all words which have *either* a prefix or a suffix.

THE NATURE AND USE OF CONTEXT CLUES

One of the most important word-recognition tools is that of context clues. Of all of the major word-analysis techniques employed in reading instruction, the use of context clues is the only one employed by many adults. There are some words such as "refuse" and "read" which require association with other words before they can be pronounced.

Many words which are normally introduced at the primary reading levels can be presented through the use of a combination sight-word–verbal-context clue approach. For example, if Bob, a slow learner, knew all of the words except *milk* in the sentence, "I want some bread and milk," the teacher might ask him what he sometimes drinks when he eats bread. If he understands initial consonant sounds, she should remind him of the sound of "m" and suggest further that since the letter "l" follows the vowel "i," the vowel sound will be controlled by the "l" sound. Using all of the approaches together will help him to unlock the word. In summary, context clues give a hint regarding the pronunciation of a word, but the accuracy of the guess must be validated through the use of other word-recognition procedures.

In using context clues, the reader must be able to pronounce and understand all, or nearly all, of the other words in the sentence. (The technique is satisfactory for a single word, but it loses its effectiveness and results in mere guessing at best when applied to several words in a sentence.) One very important principle must be remembered by the teacher of the slow learning child: context clue procedures can be used successfully if the word in question is a part of the pupil's hearing or speaking vocabulary and he has had some experience with the word. If either of these conditions are missing, another word-attack tool should be used.

Exercises for Building Competencies With the Use of Context Clues

The following exercises can be used for building competencies with the use of context clues.

1. The construction of a list of sentences with a key word omitted can help a child find suitable words through context clues. A sample list of such items might include the following:

a. Mother s — — — — the floor with her new broom.

a. He took the b — — and hit the ball.

c. "F — — —!" said Billy, as he saw smoke coming from the house.

d. Mother baked a c — — — for the children to eat.

e. You should never cross the s — — — — — when cars are coming.

For a variation of the above exercise, leave a blank for all missing letters of the desired word. At the end of the sentence, list three or four words. One of the listed words would be the most obvious choice.

2. A three-paragraph story could be duplicated and a dozen key words left out. At the close of the selection, enumerate the words in scrambled form and ask each child to place the correct word on the correct blank in the story. (Words selected for the exercise should be those which can be used in only one place in the story.)

3. The study of synonyms and antonyms is an important word-skill–building technique. The following are sample sentences from an exercise of this type.

Directions: Underline the word which means the same, or about the same, as the key word.

a. *brook*   river, stream, pond, lake
b. *fast*   slow, careful, quick, under
c. *listen*   hear, run, stop, catch

Directions: Underline the word which means the opposite of the key word.

a. *stop*   slow, halt, walk, run
b. *under*   over, high, top, side
c. *good*   pretty, ugly, nice, bad

4. Since there are a number of words which must be seen in context before they can be pronounced, each child should have practice pronouncing the words in various sentence settings. Some of the sentences which might be used for this purpose are as follows:

a. The men hauled the *refuse* to the junkyard.
   "I *refuse* to do the work," said the man.
b. Most children can *read* this sentence.
   Have you *read* many books this year?
c. There are many *lead* mines in this country.
   Dogs can help *lead* blind people.
d. "I see a *tear* in your eye," said Mary.
   Don't *tear* paper before you hand it to your teacher.
e. I *wound* the string around the stick before I knew it.
   The soldier suffered a deep chest *wound* in the battle.
f. "I will tie a *bow* in your hair," said Janie.
   The conductor said, "*Bow* at the close of your number."

THE USE OF THE DICTIONARY AS A WORD-ATTACK TOOL

There are a number of companies listed in the appendices of this volume which publish graded series of dictionaries for use at the various grade levels. In most instances, these volumes contain such features as pronunciation keys, pictures and illustrations, and easy-to-read print. Each child should have a desk dictionary which is readily available to him. For primary children, the use of a picture dictionary is very wise.

A number of teaching principles should be kept in mind with respect to instruction in the use of the dictionary with slow learners. These are enumerated below.

1. *Direct, formal instruction in the correct use of the dictionary should take place as early as the second grade.* Pupils should be taught the processes of finding words through the alphabetizing method. They should understand that there is more than one meaning to some words and that a choice of the meaning must be determined on the basis of the contextual setting of the word in a given sentence.

2. *Young children should be encouraged to make their own picture dictionaries by pasting pictures in a scrapbook to illustrate the definitions of new words which they find.* These words should be those which arise naturally from experience stories which the children have created as well as those which appear in their class printed materials. If pictures cannot be found which seem suitable for a particular word, the definition can be carefully explained and students should be encouraged to create drawings which would be illustrative of the meaning.

3. *Location skills such as learning how to use the guide words at the top of the dictionary pages should be emphasized at all levels.* Guide words represent an important feature of dictionaries, and those pupils who cannot use the aid waste much time in finding words. Primary pupils must, of course, have precise skills in alphabetizing words before trying to make use of the guide words. Knowledge of structural analysis skills which includes an understanding of all the variant words which might be formed from a common base word is important. As an example, if the child finds the word "case" as a guide word at the top of a page, he should expect to find the word "casing" further down the same page.

4. *Thorough training in the use and importance of pronunciation skills such as the meaning of key words, accent marks, diacritical markings, and phonetic spellings should precede extensive use of dictionaries which contain these aspects.* Teachers must understand that all markings found in the dictionary are necessary for the correct pronunciation and meaning which should be ascribed to a

given word. Lessons in the correct use of the dictionary should be devised for pupils. Some examples of the exercises which might be used are included in the next section.

Lessons for Teaching Dictionary Skills

1. Presuming that each child in a given class knows the alphabet and can list words in alphabetical order, the use of speed drills for finding given words can be used with success. Supply each child with a dictionary which is suitable for his grade or level and ask each of them to see who can find the correct pronunciation and meaning for given words. For example, the teacher might say, "The word is 'amuse.' See who can be first to find the word and give us the correct definition. Ready, go!"

2. A dictionary lesson exercise might be compiled with the following types of requests:

   a. On what page can one find the definition of the word "infinite?"
   b. Of the three meanings listed on page 132 for the word "substitute," copy the one which would apply in the sentence, "The coach used a substitute."
   c. How many syllables does the word "analytically," contain?
   d. What part of speech is the word "cogged?"
   e. According to your desk dictionary, what would be a suitable synonym for the word "topic?"

3. The dictionary can be used to determine if a given word has been spelled correctly. With this in mind, practice sheets can be duplicated with exercises of the following type duplicated:

Directions: In each of the following exercises, there are two words which are listed. One is not spelled correctly. Circle the incorrect word. Use your dictionary to help you.

a. symbol	cimbol	e. clear	cliar
b. control	controll	f. genurate	generate
c. diseases	disesaes	g. mitey	mighty
d. notise	notice	h. buoy	bouy

General Suggestions for Teaching Word-Recognition Skills

There are a number of admonitions which should be remembered by the teacher of slow learners when developing plans for teaching basic word attack skills. In summary, they are as follows:

1. A careful study must be made of the word-attack competencies which should be attained by pupils who have a certain potential level and are at a given chronological level. Precise evaluative techniques should be applied in order to discover what strengths and deficiencies a given child might possess at any particular moment. Remedial lessons should be planned to upgrade areas of limitation.

2. Each child must be dealt with in an individual manner when planning word-attack lessons. Some pupils need much more phonics training than do others; therefore, group methods prove to be boring for some and too difficult for others.

3. Slow-learning children need much repetitive practice in skill areas. The lessons should be of a concrete manner and contain a variety of situations. Deadening drill should be avoided.

4. Teachers should make a thorough study of the many kinds of interesting and fascinating teaching materials which are available for instruction in such areas as phonetic and structural analysis. The names and descriptions of many of these aids can be found in the appendices of this volume. Instructors should remember that no one material or technique represents a panacea for all problems.

5. The inductive, *not* the deductive, approach should be used to teach principles of word attack. "Discovering" information through a study of examples is much more meaningful and practical than having the information presented as a rule to be remembered.

6. Pupils must be taught to take the global approach to word attack by using phonetic generalizations, structural analysis, context clues, and other tools in a simultaneous manner.

7. Specific word-attack lessons (such as phonics training) should always be a part of the regular reading lesson period. Isolated drill-type lessons and activities which are apart from the reading lesson have little justification except in a strictly remedial situation where a child has a demonstrated need for such activities.

REFERENCES

1. Karlin, Robert: *Teaching Elementary Reading*. New York, Harcourt, 1971, p. 141.
2. Clymer, Theodore: The utility of phonic generalizations in the primary grades. *The Reading Teacher, 16*:252–258, 1963.
3. Smith, Nila B.: *American Reading Instruction*. Newark, International Reading Association, 1965.
4. Flesch, Rudolph: *Why Johnny Can't Read*. New York, Harper, 1955.
5. Cushenbery, Donald C.: *Reading Improvement in The Elementary School*. West Nyack, Parker, 1969, pp. 69–70. Reprinted by permission.
6. Dechant, Emerald: *Diagnosis and Remediation of Reading Disability*. West Nyack, Parker, 1968.
7. DeBoer, John and Dallman, Martha: *The Teaching of Reading*. New York, Holt, 1964.
8. Bond, Guy L. and Tinker, Miles A.: *Reading Difficulties: Their Diagnosis and Correction*. New York, Appleton, 1967.
9. Dawson, Mildred A. and Bamman, Henry A.: *Fundamentals of Basic Reading Instruction*. New York, McKay, 1963, pp. 158–159. Reprinted by permission.

Chapter VI

CONSTRUCTING A PROGRAM OF COMPREHENSION FOR THE SLOW LEARNER

DONALD C. CUSHENBERY

The ability to derive significant facts, principles, and generalizations from printed material is one of the most important competencies which a child must gain in learning to read. Some pupils can demonstrate proficiency in word calling, but they may fail in their efforts to read and interpret complex selections which involve such higher comprehension processes as differentiating between fact and opinion.

The reading instructional program which is devised by teachers and administrators is a very significant factor in the success (or failure) pattern of a given child in the area of comprehension. The suggestions and discussions which are included in this chapter are designed to aid the teacher in her efforts to build a program of comprehension which is global in nature and can be adapted to meet the needs of the slow-learning child.

SKILLS NECESSARY FOR EFFECTIVE COMPREHENSION

Numerous factors are involved as prerequisites to the act of comprehending the meaning of the printed page. Some of these aspects, such as word-analysis ability, reading purpose, and experiential and educational background, are described in the next section.

Word Analysis Ability

Before any pupil can gain information from his reading, he must be able to unlock both simple and complex words in an easy, confident manner in both oral and silent reading situations. If maximum understanding is attained, he must, of course, be able to attach meaning to the words and use them appropriately as a part of his spoken vocabulary.

Each child should be evaluated continuously to determine if he has adequate mastery of the principles involved in the use of phonetic and structural analysis, context clues, and the dictionary. If serious deficiencies are noted, remedial measures must be undertaken to correct them *before* serious attention is given to building lessons that are designed to introduce and strengthen the various comprehension skill strands which are described later in this chapter. One must keep in mind at all times that word recognition is the center or core of the reading act, and few, if any, reading skills can be taught if abilities are not developed in this area.

Reading Purpose

One of the most common reasons for limited success in grasping details and finding main ideas is general lack of reason or purpose for reading. If a sixth-grade teacher asks her pupils to merely "read" a chapter in a book and be prepared to discuss it, he or she is doing an educational disservice to the child. Every reader needs one or more guiding questions for consideration before he engages in silent reading. Without these purposes, he is likely to overlook certain important facts and may have a very low level of understanding of the total body of information which he was supposed to learn from his silent reading experiences.

For slow-learning children, the use of questions is most urgent, since they need very specific directions before they actually begin to read. The following description illustrates how one teacher developed reading purposes with a group of fourth-grade children who were studying a social studies unit.

The unit was entitled "The Land Down Under," and a large number of books at varying reading abilities had wisely been provided by the teacher. One set of common materials which was written at the fourth-grade level was available for all students. (Approximately 60% of the students could read these books with at least 75% level of comprehension.) Additional materials which were written at varying reading levels were also available for some of the students.

Miss Williams (the teacher) wrote two questions on the chalkboard which concerned the crops and people of Australia. She asked the pupils to turn to Chapter 2 of the text and note the names of the topics and subtopics which were included in the chapter. She said to the children, "What are some questions which you think we should place on the board?" Three questions were elicited from the pupils and these were added to the two which had previously been constructed by the teacher. The five questions served as the purposes for reading the unit reading matter. (If these pupils had been told, "read the chapter on Australia and we'll discuss it," very few concepts would have been learned, since they would not have had clear purposes for reading.)

Experimental and Educational Background

If the reader is to gain a clear idea of the message which an author is trying to convey, he must be able to attach some meaning to the words which are printed. For example, if a child has always lived in a large city and has never visited a farm, he would not have a complete understanding of how a mechanical corn picker works, even though his class textbook contains a lengthly description of the object. To gain a total picture of the equipment, he would have to see the picker in operation, ride on it, and touch it.

The lack of experiential background is especially common with many disadvantaged children. If a high level of comprehension is to be attained with this type of learner, the teacher must be in a position to offer rich experiences such as field trips and film presentations which will help to fill the educational void that may exist. In every conceivable way, meaning must be attached to words.

An experience which the authors had recently with a group of disadvantaged middle-grade pupils will serve to illustrate the importance of the previous concepts.

In this particular instance, a field trip was taken to the local airport. While boarding the tour bus at the close of the day, Harold stumbled over a tall red metal object that was located in the corner of the lawn. The teacher-leader admonished the child to always watch for the *hydrants* when walking. A look of obvious surprise came over his face and finally he remarked, "So that's a hydrant!" He had said the word many times, but apparently had never known the meaning of it.

With regard to the significance of the foregoing aspect, Harris and Sipay[1] offer this advice to those teachers working with slow children:

> In view of their difficulties with abstract ideas, important concepts need to be carefully developed from ample experiences and illustrations, and the meanings that these children arrive at need to be checked; they often resort to memorizing verbal formulations that they do not understand. Whenever possible, concepts should be related to practical concrete experiences that fall within the children's experiences.

THE ROLE OF COMPREHENSION IN THE TOTAL READING PROGRAM

In order to help all pupils develop maximum ability in the complex area of comprehension, a thorough understanding must be gained concerning the processes and components that are involved. The following principles have been constructed to fill this need.

Comprehension does not involve a single skill, but rather a body of complex skills which encompass such areas as details, main ideas, following directions, sequence of events, and facts and opinions. Because of this reality, each teacher needs to gear her questioning techniques to insure that each child will gain practice in something else besides the mere recitation of isolated rules and statements which may or may not be germane to a given situation.

Reading materials must be at a child's instructional or independent reading level if he is to acquire an appropriate level of understanding. Satisfactory meaning acquisition of any printed matter will not be realized unless the reader can pronounce at least 95 per cent of the words aloud and can demonstrate a minimum level of 75 per cent comprehension when many different types of questions are asked. Since some studies indicate that as many as two thirds of some school populations are being asked to read frustration-level material, the importance of this concept must not be minimized.

Comprehension skills should be mastered in sequential order in the elementary school by both normal and slow-learning children. If this condition is to be met, primary teachers should stress such aspects as reading for details and finding main ideas, while middle-grade instructors should emphasize sequence of events and the higher critical reading processes. A given developmental program should contain numerous teaching opportunities for building the skill strands which are described later in this chapter.

Reading purposes should be established with pupils before they are asked to engage in the act of silent reading. Guiding questions which have been formed by the teacher, students, and textbook author should always be established. The oral questioning techniques which are used by the teacher are also an important part of this concept. If, for example, the teacher insists on asking questions which involve only details, then the pupils will get the idea that they need to dissect and remember a vast amount of facts if they are to succeed in pleasing the teacher. They will not bother with the higher comprehensions levels such as reaction and critical reading because the teacher never asks them to read in this manner.

Every teacher reading this volume should remember that *at least 90 per cent* of the details learned by the typical student are forgotten within a short period of time after he leaves school and only the more significant main ideas are remembered. The constant and unrelenting pushing of the student to remember a myriad of facts will be of little help to him so far as his total education is concerned.

Commercial and informal tests and techniques should be used on both a periodic and a continuous basis to evaluate each child's progress in learning the comprehension skills which have been introduced and taught at his grade level. Since one of the most important goals of any testing program is to discover if reading objectives are being fulfilled, the result of instruments can be used to alter the reading program, so that more reading growth can be realized on the parts of the total student body and individual students. Facts and figures derived from such tools and techniques can also provide useful information for important school studies.

COMPREHENSION-SKILL DEVELOPMENT FOR THE SLOW LEARNER

As noted earlier, comprehension consists of a number of different skills and depends upon many factors. In some instances the reader may wish to secure only a general impression or an idea, while on other occasions his objective might be that of obtaining a host of related details about a particular subject. In any case, he must have his intention well in mind and the teacher must be in a position to help him pursue his goal. In the section which follows, a number of comprehension-skill areas are noted and appropriate suggestions are outlined for the teacher in helping each pupil derive maximum meaning from the printed page.

Obtaining the Main Idea

One of the most common purposes for reading is that of obtaining a general notion or idea which is described in a selection. Fictional-type reading or reading a newspaper is usually done with this goal in mind. Securing ideas is one of the most difficult skills to develop, since it is contingent upon the ability to remember details and place them into a general context. Meaningful lessons must be formulated for each child to insure that proficiency is obtained in this area. Some classroom-tested activities which have been used successfully with slow-learning children are included in the next section.

1. Have pupils read a short selection of three or four pages which is written at the instructional reading level of the pupils involved. Submit a list of sentences on a separate sheet of paper and ask them to find the one statement which best expresses the main idea of the passage.

2. After the students have read a short story, invite them to paint or color the one scene which expresses the major event which took place in the selection.

3. Read a story aloud to the pupils and ask them to select the one best title from a list of suggestions which has been prepared on sheets of paper. Discuss with the children the reasons why certain titles are not appropriate.

4. Orient the students to look for such words and phrases as "in summary," "finally," and "in the first place" for possible cues to main ideas which may be found in a particular paragraph or story.

5. Duplicate a three- or four-paragraph selection which is factual in nature and is of interest to the majority of the learners involved. Include a sentence in the context of the selection which expresses clearly the main idea of the passage. Ask students to underline the one sentence which is most appropriate for this purpose.

Locating Significant Details

The ability to locate and remember details requires slow, word-by-word, phrase-by-phrase reading, along with the ability to classify and retain facts and figures which might relate to a given subject. The child needs to grasp the concept of knowing what pieces of information are important for the objective he is pursuing. This skill is a difficult one for many slow learners, particularly if they are trying to assimilate a large amount of material at any given time.

Definite sequential practice with appropriate selections must be provided for each pupil so he can understand and realize the importance of details in formulating a main idea, differentiating between a fact and an opinion, or solving a problem in mathematics or science. If an adequate level of skill in remembering details is attained, careful attention must be given to training pupils to have a purpose for reading in materials which are at their instructional or independent reading levels. Teachers may wish to use one or more of the following exercises for aiding students in skill development in this important area.

1. Duplicate a three- or four-paragraph selection which might appear in a science or mathematics textbook. Ask pupils to underline all of the facts or ideas which are important in solving the problem or experiment. Show them the teacher's copy which has been prepared on an overhead projector. Comparisons can be made which will help them to understand why certain words constitute important details.

2. A number of questions can be formulated and given to each child. From a list of scrambled facts which have been compiled from a short selection, he is asked to match the fact with the question.

3. A picture of a familiar scene can be held before a group of pupils, and each of them should either write or describe orally all of the important details which they note. Encourage them to use descriptive words, mathematical sizes, and comparative language.

4. Compose a short set of directions for making a simple object which is part of a class activity. Supply each child with a copy of the directions and lend no further help either orally or written. See if he can complete the project properly according to the information which has been supplied.

5. Pose a problem which has arisen as a natural outgrowth of a lesson in science or other subject area. (An example might be the construction of a simple greenhouse for the sprouting of corn plants.) Ask pupils what kinds of information are needed for developing the project.

Following Directions

The one comprehension skill which has not been developed adequately by thousands of children, as well as adults, is that of learning to follow both printed and oral directions. Adults fail to complete income tax forms correctly, graduate students use the wrong symbols for true-false examinations, and technicians use inappropriate components in constructing a new piece of equipment. Many of these persons either ignored the training they received in school in the development of this skill or they were not exposed to the proper lessons during their school experiences.

To follow directions properly, the pupil must give close attention to each word and form a mental picture of the details. Teachers must be careful to relate directional exercises to those activities which are real and meaningful to the child. He must see the need for developing the skill and understand that if he cannot follow directions properly, he will ultimately miss many of the opportunities which will be provided for the other learners who are adept in this area.

Listening skills must be developed carefully, and the complete attention of all children must be attained, even if it is for a brief period of time. They must be given a purpose for listening and learn to expect that certain facts will be presented in some sequential order.

The directions which are given to a slow learner should be very limited in number. It is much better to derive complete proficiency in following a few commands than it is to try to develop competency in dealing with a mass of information which may not be significant to a given child.

Some activities for teaching pupils to follow directions are the following.[2]

1. With primary children, many directions should be written on the chalkboard such as "Put your books in your desk," "Pick up all of the crayons," or "It is time for recess."

2. Ask various pupils to read announcements to their fellow classmates and observe which pupils are able to follow the directions contained in the announcements.

3. A number of individual directions should be printed on one large sheet. Each pupil is to find the direction relating to him and perform the duty requested.

4. Except for a brief introduction of the purpose for a given exercise, pupils should always be expected to read and follow the directions. If the directions state that a "T" should be placed before all true statements and a child places a plus sign instead, all of these statements should be scored as being incorrect. Initially the pupil may feel this is a harsh practice; however, an impression will be made regarding the importance of following directions precisely.

5. The directions for a given activity may be printed in a "scrambled" sequence. Each student should be asked to place the statements in proper order.

6. Learning to follow directions accurately can be emphasized through the use of game activities such as the following:

Read all of the following directions accurately before completing any exercise.

a. Write the third letter of your last name in the following space
....

b. Stand and say your first and last name. (Continue similar directions until at least twenty items have been compiled. For the last item write: "Make no marks on this side of the page. Write your name on the back and give the sheet to your teacher.")

7. Brief directions can be given orally for performing an experiment or making a project. Pupils should be asked to write the directions from memory. Papers should be exchanged, and various students should be asked if they can follow the directions which are written.

Reading to Establish Sequence

Many situations develop in reading for meaning which call for the proper classification of events and situations. The understanding of how our country has developed or how to make a certain product is contingent upon a clear concept of the events and procedures involved. Fictional stories can be appreciated only after the sequence of activities which has taken place in the selections are fully grasped.

Typically, slow-learning children have difficulty with this type of skill, since it entails the remembering of a number of details along with the mental cataloguing of such facts. Teachers can do much to help them develop proficiency in this area. The suggestions listed below have been used successfully in a number of school situations by the writers.

1. Alert pupils to take note of such words as *first, second,* and *finally* when they are reading. These words are important cues to event sequences.

2. Read a brief selection aloud which includes a number of events. Duplicate a list of the events in scrambled order and ask the children to place them in proper order. Approximately four to six statements should be used for this purpose.

3. An alternate to No. 2 is the formation of three lists of sentences. One list is correct, while the other two constitute scrambled items. The reader is to select the column which represents the correct statements.

4. Comic strips can be used to build sequence of events. Select a story which is of interest to most of the pupils. Paste each story segment on a small piece of oaktag and place them on a table in a mixed order. See if one or more students can rearrange them in correct sequence. The exercise can be made self-corrective by placing the sequence number on the back of the card. Dozens of games can be constructed and used during free-reading periods for practice.

5. The demonstration of a simple science experience can be conducted for the entire class. Class members can be trained to detect the three (or more) important steps which are necessary for the development of the project. Consultations among pupils can take place to determine if all steps have been included and if they are in the correct order.

Reading Critically

As a general statement, the ability to determine the relevancy and truthfulness of a given sentence or paragraph is not well developed among the vast majority of elementary- and high-school students. For the most part, the average reader assumes that printed material found in the daily newspaper or magazine is factual and is not to be challenged.

A high level of proficiency in critical reading demands that the reader have a broad background of understanding with regard to the topic under consideration. He should compare the statements found in one source with those found in another journal or book. The background of the writer is carefully scrutinized and his qualifications for writing in a particular field are noted.

Through skillful training a teacher can help pupils develop a satisfactory level of competency in critical reading. Slow learners can be helped in this area through the use of one or more of the following exercises.

1. Duplicate a list of statements which contain both facts and opinions and ask pupils to determine the correct answers by marking "F" for fact and "O" for opinion. Some statements which might be used are:

    a. Alaska has more land area that any other state in the United States.

    b. Topeka is the capitol of Kansas.

    c. A large house is cooler than a small house during the summer months.

    d. The best schools are found in the northern part of the state of California.

    e. Dogs make better pets than cats.

    f. The name of my school is ....

2. Ask pupils to determine the statements which are not relevant in the following story. (Similar stories of more or less difficulty can be used depending on the age and aptitude of the pupils involved.)

> John went to the circus one afternoon to see the elephants dance and play tricks. Some elephants did not want to perform and sat down on the canvas. The night was black and scary. He had a good time watching all of the animals during the show and wished there was a circus show every day. At the end of the show he bought a sack of popcorn and went home. Mother washed the kitchen floor.

3. Students should be taught to look for words which arouse emotion and cause people to make sudden reactions such as love, anger, or hostility. Ask them to indicate such words in regular textbook material or in specially prepared exercises which have been supplied.

4. Train pupils to compare copyright dates and inquire about the background of the authors of source books. An exercise which would entail items such as the following may be useful for this purpose.

    a. If you wanted to find the best source of information for learning about the methods used for mining coal, which of the following books would you probably use?

        _____ MINING COAL (copyright 1971) by Dr. Theodore Adams, geologist.

        _____ KNOW YOUR MINERALS (copyright 1959) by James R. Seesay, writer.

        _____ COAL WILL NOT BURN! (copyright 1960) by Roy R. Adams, cleaning specialist.

5. Display different parts of the newspaper such as the sports page, front-page news stories, and the editorial page. Discuss the importance of each section and convey to the pupils that some parts of the paper are meant to be factual, while others represent the opinion of the editor or a columnist.

EVALUATING COMPREHENSIVE ABILITIES

As noted in Chapter IV, there are a number of procedures which the teacher can use to evaluate any given child's ability in the various comprehension skill areas which have been discussed in the previous section. The use of the informal reading inventory or a commercial instrument such as the *Durrell Analysis of Reading Difficulty* or *Gates-McKillop Reading Diagnostic Test* represents effective means for finding useful information.

After the testing information data have been classified, the use of any of the exercises noted in this chapter may be used. Many commercial devices and materials which are described in Chapter IX may be used profitably with a large number of pupils. The major task for the teacher is finding the most appropriate aid for use with a particular child who has carefully defined comprehension deficiencies.

REFERENCES

1. Harris, Albert J. and Sipay, Edward R.: *Effective Teaching of Reading.* New York, McKay, 1971, p. 399.
2. Cushenbery, Donald C.: *Reading Improvement in The Elementary School.* West Nyack, Parker, 1969, p. 94. Reprinted by permission.

Chapter VII

TRAINING IN PERCEPTUAL MOTOR SKILLS

KENNETH J. GILREATH

O f what importance to the teacher of reading is a knowledge of perception? There can be little doubt that success in learning depends heavily on the perceptual ability of the student. The successful student must be able to glean information from his environment. He must then be able to remember the information, associate it, and feed it back in an acceptable manner. Perception, then, is the mental interpretation of the messages received through the senses. The senses most involved in learning are the following:

1. *Visual perception,* the mental interpretation of what a person sees.
2. *Auditory perception,* the mental interpretation of what a person hears.
3. *Tactile perception,* the mental interpretation of what a person experiences through the sense of touch.
4. *Kinesthetic perception,* the mental interpretation of the sensation of movement.

The senses of smell and taste are also perceptual, although they are not as important in the educational process as are the others.

It should be pointed out that a given stimulus will sometimes trigger incorrect perceptions. The sound of a tractor may be recognized correctly by a child with a rural background, while a city child may fail to recognize the stimulus. Another example of perceptual errors resulting from experience might be that of a city child who viewed a pasture and grazing cattle. He remarked, "Look, Daddy, a whole lawnful of cows." Age often influences our perceptual process. An example of this might be that of a preschooler who wrote his name, Jack, with the J reversed. When his name was printed correctly and his error pointed out, he explained that he thought that the letters should all point to the right. His problem was not visual but rather a mistake in attempting to apply logic to the alphabet.

THE DEVELOPMENT OF PERCEPTION

Piaget[1] tells us that perception is developmental in nature; i.e. that it changes significantly with age and experience. Its development is continuous and quantitative. The development of perception occurs in three major periods. The first period, sensorimotor intelligence, occurs during the period between birth to 2 years and concerns itself with learning to coordinate various perceptions and movements. The second period, preparation for and organization of concrete operations, deals with the acquisition of language and occurs during the ages of 2 to 11 or 12. During this period, the child learns to deal logically with his surroundings. The third period, formal operations, occurs after the age of 11 or 12 and is concerned with the development of abstract and formal systems.

Piaget also points out that the perception of a young child is centered in the visual area and that as the child matures, it begins to decenter. A good example of how this process affects the teaching of reading can be found in a study by Elkind.[2] A figure of a man was made out of fruit. The legs were bananas; the body, a pear; the head, an apple; and the arms were made from bunches of grapes. When preschoolers were shown the picture, they saw only the fruit parts; kindergarten children saw only the man; children at the second-grade level were able to see both the fruit parts and the whole man. Because reading success depends on the ability to see parts as well as wholes (letters and words, words and sentences), it is apparent that this type of perceptual training would be a great asset to success in reading.

Perceptual Training

The slow-learning child can gain much from a regular program of sensori and perceptual training. An excellent example of such a program follows.*

---

* From Ashlock, Patrick and Stephan, Alberta: *Educational Therapy in The Elementary School*, 1967. Courtesy of Charles C Thomas, Publisher, Springfield, Illinois.

Level of Sensoriperceptual Training	*Activity*
1. *Auditory perception of dissimilar sounds.* The child learns to differentiate and perceive among dissimilar sounds.	The child is given three or four letter names and asked to select the one that is different. If the child is able to do this, work with pairs, such as pin and pen, sit and set, pick and sick, asking the child to say whether the two words are alike or different. If this task is too difficult for the child, begin training again with gross sounds such as clapping, tapping, whistling, etc. Ask the child if the sounds you are making are alike or different. When learning is solidly successful at a level, begin working up the scale until the child can perceive and differentiate among dissimilar letter names.
2. *Auditory perception of similar sounds.* The child learns to perceive and match similar sounds.	The child is given three or four letter names, two of which are the same. He is expected to select the two that are the same.
3. *Passive kinesthetic tactile.* The teacher guides the student through muscle movements and touch experiences which will form a basis for later perceptual experiences of a higher order.	The teacher takes the child's dominant hand and moves it over large alphabet letters so that the tip of the index finger touches each letter. The teacher maintains correct directionality at all times.
4. *Active kinesthetic tactile.* The child uses the sense of touch and muscle movement to perform the acts taught him at level three. The teacher supervises but does not actually move the child's hand.	The teacher gives the large alphabet letters to the child and he traces them, using correct directionality. The teacher interferes only if the child makes a mistake.
5. *Passive kinesthetic.* This is the same as level three, except that the sense of touch is no longer used. The tracing is done with a pencil, crayon, pen, etc.	The child, with the help of the teacher, traces each letter with a pencil or similar instrument. If level three and level four have been successfully passed, a minimum of time will need to be spent on level five.
6. *Active kinesthetic.* This is the same as level four, except that the sense of touch is not used. The tracing is done with a pencil or similar instrument.	The child, without the manual guidance of the teacher, traces each letter with a pencil or similar instrument. The teacher interferes only if the child makes a mistake.
7. *Visual perception of dissimilar symbols.* At this level, the child learns to perceive and differentiate among dissimilar visual symbols.	The child is given four letter forms, three of which are alike, and taught to select the one that is different.
8. *Visual perception of similar symbols.* The child learns to perceive and recognize the similarity of visual symbols.	The child is given one letter form and from three or four letter forms must select the one that matches the one given him.

Level of Sensoriperceptual Training	Activity
9. *Visual perception and kinesthetic reproduction.* At this level the child learns to perceive visual symbols and kinesthetically reproduce them.	The child looks at the letter given him and copies it with a pencil or other instrument.
10. *Visual-auditory association.* The child learns to associate visual symbols with their names.	The child is shown a letter and told its name. He is trained until he automatically says the letter name which it is shown to him.
11. *Auditory-visual association.* The child learns to associate letter names to their visual symbols.	The child is shown the letter name and is shown the letter form. He is trained until he automatically selects the correct letter form when he hears its name.
12. *Motor response to an auditory stimulus.* The child responds motorically to a verbal command.	The child is told a letter name and learns to immediately write that letter form.

Developing Visual Perception and Visual-Motor Coordination

In considering the importance of perceptual training, it must be remembered that much of our educational procedure is visual. Certainly the process of reading is visual, and the success of slow-learning children in the field of reading depends on an effective perceptual training program.

In considering visual-motor training, the teacher should begin with training in visualization. She should, at the same time, begin motoric training activities. These activities should be taught separately, as this will allow for identification (and remediation if necessary) of the individual's strengths and weaknesses in both areas. After the child's weaknesses have been identified, specific training is given to overcome them. After the program for visual training and motor training has been completed, the teacher should move on to visual-motor activities. The focus of the following suggestions will be on visual perception to visual-motor perception. An excellent source for materials and methods of motor development can be found in a number of books written by Cratty.[3]

The teacher should stress the following in each of the activities which are included in the unit: (a) background to foreground and (b) gross ability to fine ability.

Visualization Training

1. *Visual discrimination techniques promote the ability to see*

differences. Using filmstrips of familiar objects, the teacher determines the students' trouble spots, e.g. (a) directional differences, (b) detailed differences in finer shapes, (c) reversals of object positions, and (d) making generalizations from what is seen.

2. *It is usually easier for a child to understand differences than to understand the concept of likeness or sameness.* Drills with any of a number of materials (felt boards) will help to establish the "different" concept. Four identical figures are placed in a line. These figures are exactly alike except that one is a different color, e.g. three red apples and one green apple. The child is asked to identify the different one as the teacher points to each object.

The next set of four objects may be exactly alike except that one is a different shape, e.g. three red apples and one red carrot. It is very important to use small steps. If the child is unsuccessful on a trial, it may mean that the step was too large. In the example above, the steps were small; the same objects, as well as the same color, were used.

After the child has demonstrated ability to discriminate color and shape, he proceeds to differences in size, position, design, etc. Durbin[4] offers several techniques to be used when teaching the concept of "different."

Picture cards can be made by cutting out pictures from magazines and gluing them on small pieces of felt. Pictures of this kind would be more advanced than the simple figures previously discussed. Other techniques for teaching the "different" concept are as follows:

a. Hook-and-Loop board used for three-dimensional objects such as toy cars, airplanes, animals, etc.
b. Overhead projectors used with felt pictures to show shadow figures.
c. Pegboards used to show differences by varying color and position, e.g. three green pegs and one yellow peg; three pegs in a straight row and one either above or below the row.

The children may be asked to tell where the difference is—at the beginning, middle, or end. Such activities help the child in noting the initial, medial, and final differences in words later in reading.

3. *Teach the ability to see likenesses.* The same principle of using small steps applies. Using a flannelboard, bulletin board, or chalk-

board, place a simple figure on the left side of the board. A wide line is placed between the figures on the left and the others which follow it. All the figures in the line are different except one, which is exactly like the first figure. The child is asked to indicate which figure is the same as the first figure. Initially the identical figures are very different from the others, e.g. the rows might contain pictures of the following objects in this position: black horse, brown rabbit, brown rabbit, brown rabbit, black horse. Gradually the like objects will be less different from the remaining objects. As the teacher works on this concept, she will also be developing the left-to-right concept.

Another technique which develops the same concept would be to place a figure at the top of the board, with others arranged at random below it. The teacher will point to the one at the top and ask the child to find another just like it. The top object is then changed and another child is selected to match it.

4. *The child is taught likenesses and differences of geometric forms.* The same procedures are followed as previously discussed for familiar objects. The teacher first starts with differences and progresses to likenesses. Here again, small steps should be used. For example: first trial, three red circles and one blue circle; second trial, three blue circles and one red circle; third trial, three red circles and one red square. As the child advances through the lesson, the teacher can introduce other geometric forms, using the procedures previously mentioned.

5. *The recognition of geometric forms is followed by a program for developing visual perception of alphabetic symbols.* This is achieved by using the same procedures as mentioned above.

6. *The child is given training in recognizing a single pictured object and relating it to a similar one in a large scene.* A good method for this activity is to collect two copies of the same magazine, selecting two pictures and having the child match the cut-out section in one picture to its proper place in the other complete picture.

7. *Listening can be used to develop visual perception.* Using an opaque projector, pictures are viewed on the screen. One student is asked to name the objects shown; the other students are asked to raise their hands when an animal (or fruit, toys, etc.) is named. A student is then asked to name all the animals (fruit, toys, etc.) in

the picture. The other students are to listen and make any corrections that are necessary. Another adaptation of this activity would be to have the children take turns describing something in the picture.

8. *The children should learn to identify colors.* Any of a number of activities are effective in this lesson. The children might take turns describing the color of each other's clothing. For example, if Joe's shirt is described, and he is listening so that he recognizes his own clothing, he may then take a turn at describing someone else's clothes.

9. *Finer visual discrimination may be developed by matching related things.* A bulletin board, etc., may be divided vertically. Each side is labeled with such names as clothes for boys, clothes for girls, or toys and tools. The teacher then holds up pictures related to the topics, and the children are to indicate on which side of the board the item belongs.

10. *The child is encouraged to recognize visual associations.* He is presented with the following type of tasks. He is shown a fork (pictures will also work) and asked to associate it with other items. (In this case a knife and spoon). Other examples might be a hat and its association with another item of clothing or a head; a hammer and its association with other tools in the series.

11. *Focusing is important and can be stressed by using a magnifying glass.* The magnifying glass will also help to increase the child's visual attention span. Other techniques that can be used to improve focus include the following:

    a. The teacher puts several items on the board and then has a student describe one of the items. She then removes all the items except the one that the student has described. He is asked to describe it again with the rest of the class noting any differences from his first description.

    b. A projector used in a darkened or semidarkened room can help in focusing.

    c. Tachistoscopic devices are very useful in developing the ability to focus quickly and accurately.

    d. For those children who have special difficulties, blinders are sometimes helpful. These can be made by attaching pieces of cardboard to the arms of eyeglass frames. Blinders serve to limit the child's field of vision and to direct his attention to the material in front of him.

12. *To establish left-to-right directionality, many teachers utilize the comic strips of the daily newspaper.* These are familiar and motivating to the student. After the child becomes familiar with the strip, the teacher can cut them into individual pictures and have the child work on left to right directionality by arranging them in their proper sequence.

13. *Visualization can also be emphasized by asking the child to picture in his mind the subject matter which is read.* For example, if the teacher reads a sentence with the phrase "blue boat" in it, the child might be asked to visualize a boat. If the teacher reads, "Thomas ran home," he might ask the following: "Can you see Thomas run? Where did he go? How does his home look? Does it look like your home?" It will help the child to visualize if the story is discussed and unfamiliar words repeated and defined.[5]

Visual-Motor Coordination Skills

The teacher can evaluate a child's visual perception by using the *Frostig Developmental Test for Visual Perception* (see Chapter III) . Although this test is considered as a test for visual perception, motor activities are included in each of the five subtests. After having determined the student's abilities with regard to visual perception and motoric skills, a teaching program which considers his strengths and weaknesses can be planned.

The *Frostig Pictures and Patterns Program* develops five visual perceptual skills and sensory motor skills that lead to concept development and to the development of thought processes. The program consists of physical exercises, three-dimensional activities, and paper-crayon exercises.

For students who have progressed beyond the prereading readiness stages, there is the Frostig Developmental Program of Visual Perception. Activities are centered around the five perceptual areas of visual motor coordination: form constancy, eye motor coordination, figure ground, spatial relationships, and positions in space. The teacher can make the tasks easier or more difficult to suit the child's ability. A program of this type could be incorporated into daily activities and about a half hour a day should be devoted to using these materials or simulated materials with children who have special problems.

1. *Gross visual motor skills can be taught using physical-coordination activities involving gross motor and large muscle skills.* Some suggested activities are as follows:
   a. Walking on floor patterns and/or balance beams.
   b. Bouncing a ball on patterns.
   c. Bouncing a ball continuously, throwing, catching, etc.
   d. Running, skipping, hopping, etc.
   e. Playing ring-toss in a variety of games.

2. *To promote gross visual discrimination skills, simple matching exercises can be used.* The following are some examples:
   a. *Bingo fabric cards.* The teacher holds up a fabric and the children must find the corresponding fabric on their card and cover it. The first one to cover all their squares wins. This game involves visual discrimination and eye-hand coordination.
   b. *Container matching.* Various pieces of colored paper, shapes, and pictures are placed in a multiple container (egg carton works well) and the child is given a corresponding set and told to match the sets by putting the matching item in the correct compartment.
   c. *Marble sorting.* Marbles of various colors are placed in individual boxes or plates and children are given a bag of marbles with instructions to place them in the appropriate box. This activity works equally well with varieties of nails, bolts, buttons, etc.

3. *Eye-hand–coordination skills can be developed by having students locate large specified objects and putting them in a specified place.* Having children copy designs made by the teacher is also good practice. Designs can be made from mosaic tiles, buttons, pegs on a pegboard, macaroni, etc. Finger painting serves many needs, and eye-hand coordination can be developed through this activity. Also, a paint brush and a large container of water can provide hours of fun on a warm, sunny day if there is a sidewalk near the classroom. When you splash water on warm concrete, it darkens the concrete but fades quickly as the water evaporates. Thus, each child can paint with water to his heart's content.

4. *Mosaic tiles on cardboard strips can be used to develop visual discrimination of likenesses and differences.* For example, the child is asked to point to the one tile in a strip of four that is different. Eventually the child is shown four rows of tiles (four tiles in each row) and asked to identify the row that is different. These same materials can also be used to develop the concept of likeness.

5. *Picture vocabulary bingo aids language development, vocabulary growth, and eye-hand coordination.* A series of bingo cards containing pictures is made up; the teacher has a corresponding set of pictures. The teacher holds up a card and names the picture, and the child is instructed to find a square on his bingo card and cover it. Old and discarded workbooks are good sources for pictures.

6. *After the child has experienced finger painting, he is asked to copy a specified picture or design.* He will develop through finger painting to copying with crayons and paint brushes.

When the child has learned the names of things, he will be asked to group specified things. After he has grouped these objects, the teacher will question him relative to their similarities and differences.

7. *Any of a number of devices may be used to introduce the matching of alphabet letters.* The following are some examples.

a. A picture of a familiar object is pasted at the top of a sheet of paper. The name of the object is printed below the picture. The child then selects, from a group of letter cards, the beginning letter of the object.

b. Letters are placed in individual containers. The child then places all the letters that are alike in the right container.

c. Matching charts can be made for simple words. The chart might contain the names of the children in the class or safety and self-care words. The teacher holds up a small card and says the word. The child then takes the card from the teacher, says the word, and matches it with the right word on the chart.

d. The child may be given a sheet of paper with several words on it. He is also given small cards with the same words on them. He is instructed to paste the cards under their corresponding mates. Eventually the child must cut out the word and then paste, cut out each letter of the word and paste them on, copy each word, cut it out, paste it, etc.

8. *The child is taught to color, using cardboard stencils of shapes.* After he has learned to use the stencils, he can proceed to the use of forms outlined with wide, dark lines. The lines gradually get thinner and the forms to be colored become more complicated in detail. Constant attention should be given to the idea of staying within the line.

9. *Learning to use scissors should be taught.* Construction-paper strips may be pasted (by the child) at spaced intervals on white script paper. The child is shown how to hold the scissors and then attempts to cut out the strips of construction paper. Next, assistance is given to the child in cutting on wide lines drawn on construction paper. This practice teaches the child that cutting involves following lines. The lines will gradually become finer and the pattern of the lines more intricate.

10. *Puzzles of all kinds, commercial and homemade, can be used to develop eye-hand coordination.* Folding, cutting, and pasting activities are also excellent. The children should be encouraged to trace pictures and letters, using carbon paper. They should also trace some of their own pencil drawings. Coloring and painting pictures (staying within the lines) is still another activity that is effective in developing eye-hand coordination.

11. Robinson and Rauch[6] suggest some of the following visual motor coordination activities.

a. On a ditto sheet, the teacher can print rows of small geometric forms in no consistent order. The child is told to proceed from the beginning of each row and identify each figure as they occur, i.e. placing a dot in each circle. When he finishes one row, he continues by starting at the left of the next row. When he finishes identifying the circles, he starts at the beginning of the paper again, this time putting an "X" in the squares. This activity assists the child in recognizing likenesses and differences, and geometric forms. It also helps a left-to-right orientation and brings in the idea of the return sweep.

b. The child is given a catalog or old magazine with instructions to find and cut out a picture of a specified object, e.g. something that starts with the letter "b." He can then paste the picture on paper and with the teacher's help label the picture with the initial sound and the name of the object.

12. *Fine visual discrimination and visual motor coordination can be attained by using pegboards.* The teacher starts a figure or shape and asks the child to complete it. The child should be able to reproduce a figure or shape, complete pictures, or fill in missing parts. The ability to identify missing parts from pictures is another achievement that is helpful.

13. *The activity of writing in air is helpful to children who have difficulties in figure ground perception.* With her back to the class, the teacher leads the children through a series of figure and letter tracing. This is done both with eyes open and closed. The child traces large letters on the board or sandpaper letters on charts. He uses chalk to trace letters on the board.

Many of the above activities are designed for use in groups as well as for individuals. There are also several other good materials available for use with perceptual training. Materials presented by Van Witsen[7] and Avery[8] are recommended.

Teachers interested in developing the activities for perceptual training presented in this chapter would benefit from the use of the following materials:

Frostig Developmental Test of Visual Perception (Follett Publishing Co.)

Frostig Pictures and Patterns Program (Follett Publishing Co.)

Detect—A Sensorimotor Approach to Visual Discrimination (Science Research Associates, Inc.)

Overhead projector

Opaque projector

Tachistoscopic projector

Hook 'n Loop board

Pegboard

Bulletin board

Chalkboard

Matching charts

    Clothes for boys and girls

    Fabrics

    Tile

    Buttons

    Related objects

Simple words
Letters
Tactile boxes
Chalk
Small three-dimensional toys
Pictures cut from catalogs, magazines, workbooks, etc.
Magnifying glass
Comic strips
Balls of various sizes
Puzzles
Construction paper
Primary crayons and pencils
Paints
Tracing paper
Marbles
Golf tees

SUMMARY

To summarize the previous information, one might say that perception is the mental interpretation of the messages received through the senses. It is a vital cog in the reading process. The senses involved in perception, the role of perception in learning, the process of *how* an organism perceives, and the development of the perceptual process are all important factors in teaching slow learners to read effectively.

After the teacher of the slow-learning child has successfully determined the student's perceptual assets and liabilities, she will want to select activities and materials that will assist the child in developing his perceptual skills.

REFERENCES

1. Piaget, J.: *Les mecanismes perceptifs.* Paris, Presses Universitares de France, 1961.
2. Elkind, David: Piaget's theory of perceptual development: its application to reading and special education. *The Journal of Special Education,* Summer, 1967, pp. 357–361.
3. Cratty, Bryant, and Martin, Sister Margaret: *Perceptual Motor Efficiency in Children.* Philadelphia, Lea and Febeger, 1969.
4. Durbin, Mary Lou: *Teaching Techniques for Retarded and Pre-Reading Students.* Springfield, Thomas, 1967.

5. Flower, Richard; Gofman, Helen, and Lawson, Lucie (Eds.): *Reading Disorders: A Multidisciplinary Approach*. Philadelphia, Davis, 1965.
6. Robinson, H. Allen, and Rauch, Sidney J.: *Guiding the Reading Program, A Reading Consultant's Handbook*. Chicago, Science Research Associates, 1965.
7. Van Witsen, Betty: *Perceptual Training Activities Handbook*. New York, Teachers College Press, 1967.
8. Avery, Marie L., and Higgins, Alice: *Checklist for Single and Coordinated Sensori and Perceptive Activities*. Los Angeles, Marian Wolf Education Materials, 1967.

Chapter VIII

MOTIVATING THE CHILD TO READ

Kenneth J. Gilreath

A discussion of slow learners in the classroom is incomplete without a careful look at the subject of motivation. Education has progressed beyond ignoring a child's success or failure. Failure in school is no longer considered a responsibility of the child but rather a problem directly attributed to the teacher and/or the school. The classroom teacher—indeed the entire school system—must now look very closely for the reasons why so many of their students are having difficulty in school. If motivation is to facilitate learning, it is important that teachers know what it is and how it can be most effectively utilized in assisting slow learners.

DEFINITION

The *Dictionary of Education*[1] offers this definition of motivation:

> The practical art of applying incentives and arousing interest for the purpose of causing a pupil to perform in a desired way; usually designates the act of choosing study materials of such a sort and presenting them in such a way that they appeal to the pupil's interests and cause him to attack the work at hand willingly and to complete it with sustained enthusiasm; also designates the use of various devices such as offering rewards or an appeal to the desire to excel.

Motivation is an inner force. It is not something that can be given to a student; it is not something that can be directly observed. Motivation is a force that lies within the individual. By observing the individual's behavior, the alert teacher will be able to infer the cause of his behavior. The reason a student behaves as he does is referred to as motivation.

A good understanding of both education and psychology is necessary in order for a teacher to effectively provide learning experiences which are pertinent to a child's purposes and goals. Children who are slow to learn, whether it be because of low capacity or other reasons, fail because the program in which they are involved is inadequate. This is also true of those children who create disturbances in the classroom. The teacher needs to be aware of, and utilize, the inborn needs and desires of the children in order to effectively obtain the proper results. When the classroom situation is such that the student is able to enhance his self-concept, he will become a willing student and participate in a manner that is acceptable to the teacher, the school, and society in general.

After the normal child has been in school for two or three years, he begins to show a pattern of behavior that is fairly consistent with the objectives of proper school activity. The problem of behavior with the slow learner is that he differs greatly in some of these areas. A comparison of motivational responses of normal children and slow learners might prove helpful.

Normal Response	*Slow Learner's Response*
1. Works independently to achieve recognized goals.	1. Unless work is especially geared to his level (it often isn't), the slow-learning child will not be able to achieve satisfaction from independent work; he will be unable to reap the rewards of reaching satisfying goals.
2. Works to please teachers and parents and to meet their expectations.	2. Slow learners do not compare favorably to normal classmates and siblings, and so the expectations of teachers and parents are often beyond their ability. Realistic parent-teacher goals are needed.
3. Works under a self-inflicted fear of failure.	3. Slow learners are familiar with failure. While failure may motivate normal children to try harder, it has a debilitating effect on slow learners.

As children grow older and more experienced, they develop more complex motives. The role of the teacher and the parent become less important to their goals. The peer group, individual desires, and future plans start to take over more of the motivational conditions which affect the student's school behavior.

The size and complexity of our modern schools often impose limits within which learning and teaching are expected to occur. The many cases of overcrowded schools, rigid curricula and outdated or outmoded instruction limit educational success. If the slow-learning child is to develop adequate educational patterns, it is necessary that the school systems provide him with the kind of atmosphere that is needed to foster satisfactory growth. The school environment must also strive to be relatively free of those conditions which cause anxiety and conflict.

One of the more basic considerations in teaching slow learners to read is that of developing proper attitudes toward the reading activity. Because the slow-learning child has so often met with failure in reading, he has usually developed an attitude of withdrawal. This must be replaced with positive attitudes toward reading.

If slow learners are to experience success in the reading process, the wise teacher will want to follow a number of procedures designed to overcome his reluctance toward the subject. Reading materials selected to fit the individual's academic and interest level are regarded as essential. The teacher will also want to make the child aware of any small success or growth he achieves. Another technique which has been used successfully with slow learners is to encourage the child to compete with himself rather than with others.

DEVELOPING THE NEED TO READ

Perhaps the greatest motivational boon to the slow-learning student is for the teacher to develop within the child a *need* to read. The child who has a need to read and a teacher who will provide him with appropriate materials and proper methods will achieve surprising results. A good example of this occurs when slow learners reach the age of sixteen and are eligible for a driver's license. Because the desire to drive an automobile is so strong within these individuals, and because they recognize that reading is necessary if they are to pass the driver's examination, these students often achieve in reading where they formerly failed.

A study project with EMR children in Omaha, Nebraska, achieved excellent results by combining this need to read with materials that were specifically designed to meet the ability level of the students. Mrs. Rita Behers[2] and her colleagues adapted the Nebraska Drivers Manual into story form and simplified it so that the children could read and understand the content. A sample of the material follows:

Lesson Three

Safety Laws

Traffic laws are very important. Steve and Carol know this. They cannot be good drivers until they know the traffic laws.

Unless there is good reason, you should always stay on the *right* side of the road.

If you hear a siren, stop your car as close to the side of the road as possible. Do not stop your car in an intersection. Do the same thing if you see a flashing red light of a fire truck, police car, or ambulance.

When such a vehicle passes, do not follow until you are *500 feet* or more behind it.

Each of the twelve lessons is followed by a simplified test to allow the child to determine if he understands and remembers the content. Not only are students enthusiastic about the material but they experience success in passing their driver's examinations.

A look into the interests and activities of slow learners often gives the teacher insight into what these children will respond to in a reading program. As all boys typically do, slow learners respond to such topics as cars, mechanics, drag racing, and sports. As these students mature, they show normal interest in girls and begin to develop vocational objectives. A part-time job is often motivating, and if reading is a necessary part of the job, most slow-learning students will respond favorably. Girls have interests in scouting, household tasks, grooming, and, of course, boys. Reading motivation can be effectively achieved by utilizing these interests in preparing the reading program.

ALLEVIATING PRESSURES

There are many kinds of pressures and problems connected with school that create anxiety for even the most well-adjusted child. This is doubly true for slow-learning children. The numerous academic pressures which all school children must learn to live with are often so severe for these special children that the motivational process is blocked. It is important, therefore, for teachers of slow learners to make special efforts to eliminate these pressures. The following suggested procedures will be beneficial in assisting slow learners to succeed.

1. *The child's differences should be minimized.* It is important that the teacher treat these children as they would normal children.

They probably will not respond normally, however, and the teacher should be prepared for this behavior.

2. *Learning procedures must be repeated.* The overlearning technique is effective in developing retention, and successful experiences are motivating to slow learners. A regular program of practice and drill which is prepared for the specific learning level of the individual is desirable. This repetition is often most successful if presented in the form of a game. Numerous short lessons are usually more effective than are less-frequent longer ones. Varying the method and the materials used in these repetitive drills is also effective in motivating the child.

3. *Give the slow learner sufficient time to work.* The slow tempo of these children is characteristic. The slow learners must be given time to adjust to new situations, to think through problems, and to complete given tasks. The whole lifestyle of the individual may be leisurely. It may be necessary for the teacher to allow him to do nothing at all at times. It is more important for the child to be given sufficient time to complete an assignment than to comply with a class schedule.

4. *Goals must be set by the teacher for meeting the specific needs of individual children.* These goals must not overtax the slow learner but must be difficult enough to challenge him. The slow learner will often respond more efficiently to these goals if he understands what they are and what purpose they serve.

5. *Remember that the unknown is frightening.* The slow learner must be able to find security in his relationship with his teacher. The teacher's reassurance regarding his work, progress, and behavior will be a great asset to him. Scolding and force are not generally effective with slow learners. Anticipating and circumventing errors before they happen is more effective than correction after the mistakes occur.

BEHAVIOR MODIFICATION

No commentary on motivation would be complete without some mention of behavior-modification strategy. Teachers have long been aware that many children exhibit behavior which interferes with learning. In dealing with this behavior, the teacher is not so much concerned with the "why" of the activity as in the "what." The reasons why the child behaves as he does are not considered as important as the behavior itself.

The various interfering behaviors which children exhibit in the classroom are learned; that is, the behavior is reinforced in some manner which is rewarding to the child. Behavior modification occurs when the teacher is able to erase the interfering behaviors and replace them with activities designed to assist learning. Interfering or maladaptive behavior can be identified as any type which deviates from the expectations associated with the child's age, sex, or status. The behavior must be of such a nature that it interferes with learning and must be of a type which can be modified or changed.

Goals must be set up to achieve the modification of undesirable behavior within the classroom. Hewett[3] describes the basic goals as being the identification of maladaptive behaviors which interfere with learning, and assisting the child in developing behavior that is more conducive to learning. It is wise to observe the child closely so that one can accurately identify the things the child does that interfere with his learning process. Prescott[4] describes a method of observation which is helpful. It consists of a concentrated three-minute observation of a child involved in classroom routine. All activities are observed and recorded. This would include even the most insignificant behavior, such as foot-tapping or eye blinking. It would also include the number of times each activity occurred. All vocalization would be recorded.

In addition to goals aimed at identification of deviant behavior, it is also important to develop goals for the purpose of assisting children in the development of adaptive behavior. After the teacher has identified the behavior she wishes to change, it is necessary for her to set up a program whereby this can be achieved. This can be done in a number of ways. Let us take, for example, a child who is having difficulty staying in his seat. Following is a list of activities which will assist the teacher in modifying the child's behavior.

1. *Make the child aware of his behavior.* Many times a behavior such as this can be severely curtailed simply by having the child record the number of times in a given period of time that he leaves his seat. The record is charted and compared to previous activity.

2. *Develop in-seat activities that are rewarding to the child.* If the child is interested in what he is doing, and if he finds the activity

enjoyable, he will have less reason for wandering from his desk. Care should be taken that the lessons are within the student's range of ability and that they are educationally worthwhile.

3. *Reward the child for remaining in his seat.* If he is successful in staying at his desk for a prescribed period of time, he is rewarded in some manner. The reward can be any of a number of things, ranging from candy or tokens to teacher approval. The required period of time that the student must stay in his seat should be relatively short initially. As he experiences success, the time can be lengthened.

BEHAVIOR MODIFICATION APPLIED

The effectiveness of behavior modification can best be seen through example. What follows is a method of teaching which shows a practical application of the techniques used in behavior modification. The model is designed for use with a class comprised of slow learners but could also be used with individuals placed in regular classrooms.

Token System of Reinforcement

One of the better methods used to reinforce adaptive behavior is that of rewarding acceptable activity. Poker chips are effective and readily available. It is recommended that a monetary value be placed on the token, e.g. a white chip compares with a penny, a red chip equals a nickel, and a blue chip has a ten-cent value. In this way, the children are able to equate the chips with things of worth. The teacher then places token value on various activities within the classroom and also awards bonuses as she sees fit. At various time intervals, the chips are redeemable for purchasing items of value.

Earning Tokens

BEFORE-BELL PROCEDURE. Teachers may award tokens for any number of activities. If, for example, the children complete the before-school routine of taking care of their wraps, going to the bathroom, getting a drink, sharpening their pencils, and being in their seats at the bell, an award of five points may be given by the teacher. A five-point reward system is recommended so that the teacher can recognize the individual efforts of those who are initially having trouble. If a child can achieve only part of the before-school routine, he can be rewarded with one or two tokens. In this manner, he is experiencing some success, being reinforced through the reward, and being spurred on toward total success. As the activity becomes familiar to the class, the tokens can be phased out and replaced with verbal reward.

WORK-TIME PROCEDURE. Most teachers who work with slow learners recognize the need for individual programs for each student. The concept of behavior modification works most effectively with this program. It can, however, be effectively applied to most group studies. After the teacher decides what work behavior she feels is desirable, she may award a white token for achieving the following results:

1. Sitting at work area.
2. Raising hand rather than talking out.
3. Starting work at the proper time.
4. Finishing work on time.
5. Work completed according to teacher standards of quality and neatness.

INDIVIDUAL BEHAVIOR PROBLEMS. Every classroom contains a few children with the kind of individual behavior that not only creates disturbances in the classroom but seriously retards the individual's learning. Other children may possess behavior that is socially unacceptable. These kinds of activity can easily be altered through token reinforcement. An example of this type of behavior might be the girl who has not learned to sit at her desk in a ladylike way. After the teacher has called her attention to the problem, the child begins charting the activity and keeping a record of her success. The teacher awards bonus tokens for success. This kind of problem is rapidly corrected and the tokens can be quickly phased out.

Graphing

One of the most important aspects of the behavior-modification procedure is that of accurately charting the program. A child who is involved in recording his activity, either by himself or with his teacher's help, achieves several benefits. First, he becomes very aware of the frequency of his actions. This is particularly important if the child and the teacher are attempting to remove a particular behavior that is interfering with the child's academic success. The child is also able to see graphic evidence of improvement. Graphs can be used effectively to display a number of the following uses:

1.   Line graphs showing percentage of correct work. This has the advantage of allowing a slow learner to compete with himself rather than other more successful class members.

2.   Bar graphs can be used to identify progress in subject areas. Children who are involved in activities that require improvement in competence, such as reading skills or mathematical concepts, can be highly motivated by a graph.

Use of the Token System

The token system gains much of its effectiveness from the fact that the teacher has developed motivating uses for the tokens that the children have earned. Individuals respond because of interest factors which are stimulating to us personally. The token gives the child an immediate reward. It further allows him an opportunity to purchase worthwhile items at a later time. This "saving up" of tokens teaches the child economy. It also teaches him to delay his reward, thus allowing him to function more effectively in the classroom where many of the better rewards are delayed. Some effective examples of how the child can use the tokens follow.

Purchase of Free Time

Many teachers allow children to buy free time with the tokens they have earned. This is especially effective if the tokens were earned for such things as completing their work on time while achieving a certain level of quality. It is also suggested that the teacher provide an approved recreational area where this time can be spent. A transistor radio or record player equipped with earphones are popular ways for children to spend their free time.

Purchase of Privileges

There are several types of activities within the school setting which are popular with students and which can be classified as privileges. Within the classroom itself, the teacher is able to provide opportunities for popular and motivational activities. A corner of the room can be set aside for a game table. The games, if properly selected, can be educational in nature and will also be popular if they are saved for special occasions. If it is possible to establish an agreement with the librarian so that the children can earn the *right* to use that facility, many worthwhile educational objectives can be accomplished. Another valuable educational experience can be achieved if the teacher can acquire an adding machine and a typewriter for her classroom. The mechanical attractiveness of these machines is motivating, and many children will choose to spend their tokens for the privilege of using them. A few minutes of extra time at recess or the right to be the "leader" of the various recess activities are other attractive things for which the tokens can be spent.

There are also a number of activities within the school which are popular and can serve as privileges. Various "fun" films are available, and the right to view them can be purchased. The students can also buy the right to attend such functions as programs presented by other classes and such special parties as are held at birthdays, Christmas, and Halloween. The principal can get into the act by making available various school supplies such as pencils, construction paper, and erasers to the students who wish to use their tokens in that manner. This would give the student an opportunity to visit the principal's office under the most pleasant circumstances rather than for punishment, as is so often the case. By praising the student for his earnings, the principal could act as a strong reinforcer.

Special Contracts

For those children who are plagued with a particular problem, the idea of a special contract is often effective. The teacher and the child get together to discuss the problem. After agreement is reached as to what the procedures and goals are, the teacher and the student sign a contract with which they both agree to comply. A certain number of tokens are awarded for the prescribed and agreed-upon activity. If John, for example, is able to stay in his seat; if he is quiet and busy, the teacher reinforces him with a certain number of tokens. She should also award unscheduled bonus tokens if the child is experiencing unusually good results. This type of contract is effective for correcting such habits as talking out, wandering around the room, and thumbsucking. It is also effective in developing good grooming habits.

Loss of Tokens

Under certain circumstances, taking tokens away seems to be beneficial. The loss of tokens usually should be agreed upon beforehand and should be done in such a manner that the child is aware that if he misbehaves in a certain manner he will lose some of the tokens that he has previously earned. If the children are aware that they will lose a white chip if they fail to return their chairs to the proper place or if they do not complete their assignments because of wasting time, they soon correct the situation.

These are a few of many techniques which can be used successfully to modify behavior. The concept of behavior modification works with both individuals and groups and is basically concerned with the process of identifying the problems that exist, agreement by the student and the teacher as to the desirabiliy to change, and planning together the proper method of achieving the change. The selection of valuable rewards is also important if the program is to succeed.

MATERIALS FOR MOTIVATING THE SLOW LEARNER TO READ

Because reading is such a vital part of the total educational program and because it is so often troublesome for the slow learner, it is imperative that reading motivation be at the maximum. It has been pointed out in previous chapters that special methods are effective with the slow-learning reader. One aspect of the value of such methods as games, contests, and puzzles is that they provide the much-needed motivation for learning the material contained within these activities. It has also been mentioned previously that teacher-made materials are motivational for the slow learner. There are also a number of commercially prepared programs which are especially designed to assist the slow learner.

Stanwix House, Inc.[5] has published a developmental reading program of materials designed specifically for mentally retarded and slow learning children. The program incorporates many motivational factors which are helpful in teaching reading to slow-learning students. The series is designed as an individual progress procedure and has been developed to fit a number of various mental and academic levels.

Another reading program which has been successful with students experiencing reading difficulty is the *Sullivan Series*.[6] This program begins with a series of letters and short words and is described as being both developmental and remedial. It provides the added advantage of self-checking after each answer. Slow-learning children find this technique (programmed learning) valuable and motivating.

It is also helpful to supplement the regular reading program with materials that are designed to increase interest. The high-interest, low-level materials mentioned previously serve well for this purpose. *The Checkered Flag Series*,[7] *New Reading Skill Builder* (see Chapter IX), and *Teen-Age Tales* (see Chapter IX) are all effective supplements to the student's regular reading program.

There are, of course, many other materials available for use in motivating the slow learner. Generally, it is considered that the most effective results will be achieved by developing short individual lessons which allow the child to experience *success* while competing with himself rather than the other more successful members of his class.

SUMMARY

In summary, motivation plays a vital role in teaching slow-learning children. Human activity results from an inner motive which rewards the individual. Because slow learners often respond rather differently to a given stimulus than do normal children, it is necessary that teachers understand the concept of motivation.

The development of proper attitudes toward school and the development of motivating materials as well as effective methods are vital to the success of slow-learning children. Providing the child with successful experiences in reading is perhaps the most motivating factor in meeting the reading needs of these children.

The successful teacher will want to give particular attention to the process of alleviating pressure and anxiety so that the child can effectively pursue his learning objectives. A program designed to assist the child in modifying his maladaptive behavior is suggested as an effective method of insuring that slow learners achieve their full potential in the field of reading.

REFERENCES

1. Good, Carter W.: *Dictionary of Education.* New York, McGraw-Hill, 1959, p. 354.
2. Behers, Rita M., Gilreath, Kenneth J., and Pierson, Marty: *Simplified Edition Nebraska Driver's Manual.* Lincoln, Nebraska, Johnsen Publishing Co., 1968, p. 12. Reprinted by permission.
3. Hewett, Frank M. *The Emotionally Disturbed Child in the Classroom.* Boston, Allyn, 1968.
4. Prescott, Daniel. *The Child In The Educative Process.* New York, McGraw-Hill, 1957.
5. *A Functional Basic Reading Series.* Pittsburgh, Stanwix House, 1968.
6. Sullivan, M. W. *Sullivan Reading Program.* Palo Alto, Calif., Behavioral Research Laboratory, 1964.
7. Bamman, Henry A. and Whitehead, Robert J. *The Checkered Flag Series.* San Francisco, Field Educational Publication, 1967.

Chapter IX

MATERIALS FOR TEACHING READING TO SLOW LEARNERS

Donald C. Cushenbery

There are literally dozens of publishers and other concerns who are presently producing materials in the area of reading for all types of pupils. Many of these aids can be useful for helping the teacher fulfill her primary and secondary instructional objectives for children in both individual and group situations. One fundamental fact must be understood at the very outset when considering which material to purchase: *there is no one book or set of materials which will supply all of the reading instructional needs for any given child.*

The most important ingredient in any outstanding reading program is an alert, innovative teacher who is sensitive to such things as each child's reading instructional level, his potential reading level, and his strengths and limitations with regard to the skills which are expected of him when his age and other factors are considered. The well-trained teacher can be helped tremendously in her efforts to achieve optimum success for each pupil by using appropriate supportive materials.

The quality and general usefulness of a given aid must be carefully evaluated in terms of a teacher's immediate and long-term instructional objectives. Some workbooks, books, and audiovisual devices are designed to help a child in a certain limited way, and this piece of information should be understood by each teacher. In the sections of this chapter which follow, the particular function for each material is described.

One of the best ways of learning about the value of a given instructional aid is to use it in a pilot program situation and weigh its advantages and limitations in an objective manner. Too many teachers and administrators are prone to order vast amounts of material only to find that it does not suit the need they had for it.

A number of questions should be answered before choices of materials are made for a given classroom or systemwide objective. Each teacher should ask:

1. To what degree do the objectives of materials match the instructional objectives for a pupil or group of pupils who need developmental or remedial teaching?
2. Are they easy to use and generally stimulating to the students?
3. Is the cost of the items within the budget which I have available for instructional materials?
4. Does the data and conclusions from reputable research studies indicate that the program can achieve results for *slow-learning* children? (Some items are very useful for average to gifted children, but have very limited value for pupils with lesser academic abilities.)
5. To what degree are the materials diagnostic in nature? Do they supply lessons and exercises to help children overcome their deficiencies?
6. Are the program components self-correcting and self-directing, or must they be completely directed by the teacher in each instance?
7. Is a testing program available with the items for checking each child's progress?
8. Is the program so constructed to make allowances for individual needs of children, or is it group oriented?
9. How much help in using the materials might be expected from the publisher's salesmen and/or consultants?
10. Is it possible to buy only one part of a kit or a program without having to buy the entire set?
11. What comments do other teachers of slow-learning children make about a particular instructional item?
12. What is the copyright date of the aid and does the company expect to revise the material in the near future?
13. What comments do local-area and national slow-learning specialists make about materials in question?

Since there is a material explosion taking place in the educational field, it is impossible to list more than a sampling of the supportive aids which are currently available. To further complicate the situation, many companies are in the process of merging, revising prices, adding materials, and eliminating other items. The reader should make inquiry regarding the very latest information about certain materials by writing to the company. The addresses for all publishers listed in the rest of this chapter can be found in the appendices.

The listing of any particular program in this or any other part of the volume does not necessarily imply personal endorsement on the part of the authors. By the same token, because a material is not listed does not mean that it is not worthy of consideration by a teacher or administrator.

An organization pattern for the listing of programs and aids has been arbitrarily made. The sections include class newspapers, general reading programs, multimedia materials, reading laboratories, and reading series.

CLASS NEWSPAPERS

Know Your World (American Education Publications).

Older pupils who have instructional reading levels at the second- and third-grade levels enjoy this weekly paper. Current news topics are written in a high-interest–low-vocabulary manner. Each issue contains suitable and meaningful practice in the areas of phonics and vocabulary.

News For You (Laubach Publishing Company).

There are two editions of this weekly paper which is written at middle-grade reading level. Current topics surrounding human interest stories are highlighted in each edition.

Scope Magazine (Scholastic Magazines).

This weekly publication has a junior-senior high school interest level with middle-grade reading difficulty. The paper provides effective material for building vocabulary and comprehension skills.

GENERAL READING PROGRAMS

The Afro-American in United States History (Globe Book Company).

This volume has a readability level of about 5.5 and is intended for junior and senior high-school students. The history of black Americans begins in Africa and proceeds through history to the present time. Original source materials are included in the text to give students some taste of the writing style and art of the time.

Building Reading Power (Charles E. Merrill).

Fifteen different study booklets designed to improve each pupil's ability in the areas of structural analysis, content clues, and general comprehension skills are included in this program. The instructional materials are especially useful for older slow learners who are reading at the middle-grade level and who need reteaching in the aforementioned skills.

Developmental Learning Materials (Developmental Learning Material Company).

Many devices are included in the aids for helping children who have orientation problems, perception difficulties, and auditory perception problems.

Gates-Peardon Reading Exercises (Teachers College Press).

These paperback booklets contain exercises which serve to strengthen a child's competency in the area of comprehension. Pupils who function at reading levels from first to seventh grade should find the series useful in helping them to predict outcomes, find details, and understand directions.

Inquiry: U.S.A. Themes, Issues, and Men in Conflict (Globe Book Company).

Suitable for use with the junior or senior high-school slow learner, this paperback text can be used profitably in American history courses. The inquiry approach of teaching is encouraged by the inclusion of opposing points of view from the media of the times. The reading level is approximately 5.5.

McCall-Crabbs Standard Test Lessons in Reading (Teachers College Press).

Reading speed and comprehension are stressed in each of the five booklets which are designed for use with pupils from grades 2 through 12. There are 28 lessons in each booklet, and stimulating multiple-choice–type questions are printed at the end of each selection to build predetermined reading skills.

Modern Reading Skilltext Series (Charles E. Merrill).

A large number of skills are emphasized in this series of books for upper-grade and senior-high use. The exercises contain lessons on exploring books; following directions; finding information; reading graphs, schedules, and tables; increasing reading speed; understanding arithmetic formulas, and interpreting advertisements. In order to provide the teacher with diagnostic information, two tests are included with each book. A large number of tapes have been constructed for use with the skilltexts. The tapes have special appeal for the slow learner.

New Reading Skilltext Series (Charles E. Merrill).

This collection of six paperback skilltexts contains many short, interesting selections, followed by meaningful exercises which are designed to develop such reading skills as enlarging vocabulary, reading for details, reading critically, arranging ideas, and unlocking strange words. The aids are to be used with pupils from grades 2 through 6. Skilltapes are available for each of the books, and a number of children can be involved in a given assignment through the use of headsets and recorder jacks.

Phonics We Use (Lyons and Carnahan).

Those pupils from grades 1 through 9 who need intensive remediation in basic phonic principles should find the seven worktexts in this series to be useful. The teacher's edition contains suggestions for using each book and also provides an answer sheet for each of the exercises. All phonetic generalizations, from initial consonants to advanced syllabication procedures, are encountered.

Reader's Digest Educational Edition (Reader's Digest Services).

This volume is the regular monthly edition of *Reader's Digest*. A student guide accompanies the journal and is constructed to help the junior and senior high-school student increase his vocabulary and comprehension skills.

Reader's Digest Skill Builders (Reader's Digest Services).

The basic *Skill Builder* series consists of paperback readers for use with pupils from grades 2 through 6 and the *Advanced Skill Builders* are for pupils reading at the seventh- and eighth-grade levels. The basic objective of the program is to help the learner build word-attack skills and improve comprehension ability.

Reading in High Gear (Science Research Associates).

This set of materials is especially helpful for the slow learner who is in the junior or senior high school and is severely deficient in all basic reading areas. The workbook series contains helpful exercises for stimulating pupils to make rapid gains in such segments as phonetic analysis and structural analysis.

The Ring 'n Key Program (Play 'n Talk International Headquarters).

Ring 'n Key makes use of a typewriter to help develop reading and spelling success. This system helps the child connect finger and muscle movements. It also aids in the development of individualized instruction and reinforces skills which he has learned. The system is suitable for grades 1 through 9. Colored key tabs are placed over typewriter keys and colored rings are placed on the child's fingers. The total procedure involves visual and tactile competencies and serves to strengthen these areas.

Vanguard School Program (Teaching Resources).

Designed to develop perceptual-motor skills, the *Vanguard* program is of general use in kindergarten and primary grades and includes developmental and remedial activities for slow learners, the perceptually handicapped, and older students. The four parts of the program include *Body Awareness, Visual-Motor Integration, Discrimination and Classification,* and *Concepts of Spatial Awareness.*

Woodland Series (Continental Press).

These materials provide reinforcement of phonic and structural analysis skills for those pupils who read at the fourth- and fifth-grade levels. The selections are easily read and the principles are presented in a sequential order.

MULTIMEDIA MATERIALS

Basic Primary Phonics and Filmstrips Series (Society for Visual Education).

There are 17 filmstrips in the collection, which involve information relating to initial consonant sounds, L and W blends, two- and three-letter blends, short and long vowel sounds, digraphs, R controller sounds, rhyming sounds, and final consonant sounds.

While the material is designed for grades one, two, and three, older children who need the reinforcement in the areas can profit from the presentations.

Dandy Dog's Early Learning Program (American Book Company).

This program is especially constructed for use with slow learners, since the materials are arranged sequentially and are easily understood. Basic reading skills are emphasized through the use of story records, storybooks, records, learning activities, practice pads, and slides. A planbook and handbook are provided for the teacher.

Imperial Instructional Tapes (Imperial Productions).

This 40-tape series is a self-teaching program designed for primary children and is built around comprehension and word-attack skills. Those pupils who need further readiness for reading can use the lessons for this purpose.

Language Master (Bell and Howell).

Special sound cards can be used with the machine to help the learner understand the sounds of words. There is a student button and a teacher button. Pupils can record their own pronunciation of words and compare them with the correct pronunciations which have been previously recorded by the manufacturer.

Plan 'n Talk Phonics Course (Play 'n Talk).

This audiovisual procedure involving the use of five records and two books in two series is constructed for the needs of primary children and older slow-learning children who need intensive instruction in phonic principles.

Sounds for Young Readers (Educational Record Sales).

Primary and middle-grade students who need a remedial help in phonetic principles involving both consonants and vowels can use these aids. Auditory discrimination can also be aided by these procedures.

READING LABORATORIES

Cenco Reading Program-Child Edition (Cenco Educational Aids).

Slow learning and disadvantaged pupils who read up to the fourth-grade level find these materials fascinating and educational. A reading pacer, student workbook, dictionary, and 14 lesson rolls constitute the basic packet of aids.

Cracking The Code (Science Research Associates).

The program is designed to make use of the linguistic patterning approach to teach basic decoding skills to middle- and upper-grade students who have missed basic word-analysis skills in their previous educational experiences. In all cases, the sound-spelling relationships with respect to whole words are emphasized. The total kit is composed of three components consisting of a selection book, a practice book, and a guide for the teacher.

Early Childhood Curriculum: A Piaget Program (Learning Research Associates).

This program provides methods and materials for developing a logical thinking process for nursery and kindergarten children. Based on Piaget's theories of classification, number measurement, and space (conservation) and seration, the material consists of three kits with actual objects for manipulation, perception, and discrimination.

The Language Communication Program (Bowmar).

This material is designed for students whose chronological ages are from 8 through 14. Language concepts and vocabulary skills are taught. It is programmed for use at the third-grade level. Each program contains picture dictionaries, trophy books, study prints, and other teaching materials. The basic content of the series is built around cars and horses.

Macmillan Reading Spectrum (Macmillan Company).

There are three basic sections of this reading-program kit. It contains six skill booklets which are self-directing and self-correcting in each of the following areas: *Word Analysis, Vocabulary,* and *Comprehension*. Since the materials are nongraded, the teacher is supplied with placement tests to provide diagnostic data for placing a given child in the right kind of lesson series. In addition to the above components, one can purchase a set of 60 elementary-level books to accompany the skills segment.

Micromedia Classroom Libraries (Xerox).

The contents of childrens' books have been put on microfiche for easy viewing and motivation. The cards are slipped into a 12 x 12 inch microfiche reader which the company describes as "childproof." The cards are available in black and white; however, some titles are in color. The readability levels range from kindergarten through the ninth grade.

Reading Attainment System (Grolier Educational Corporation).

This program is designed as a basic remedial program for those students who have instructional reading levels of from third to fourth grade but who have interest levels at the junior- and senior-high levels. Segments of the system include over 100 reading-selection cards, skill exercises, answer keys, and carefully devised student record books for recording answers and plotting progress.

Reading Incentive Program (Bowmar).

This set is a basic multimedia approach to reading. The selections are at the third grade level but the content interest is at the secondary level. Each classroom kit contains a filmstrip, recording, and ten student books along with the teacher's manual.

Ready, Set, Read! (Learning Corporation of America).

This reading readiness program contains 36 Super 8 film loops designed especially for grades kindergarten through 3 and for older children who have not mastered basic skills. Most of the films can be used with children who speak any language and also be employed without constant teacher supervision. For highly distractable pupils, this approach provides for active participation of the learner in naming, describing, predicting, and solving problems.

Speech-to-Print Phonics (Harcourt, Brace and Jovanovich).

This complete program can be used independently of other reading systems and is intended for primary pupils and those slow learners who are in the middle grades and who need this type of remedial work. A teacher's manual for the 50-lesson kit is provided, along with phonics practice cards for the teacher and response cards for pupils. The organized procedures of helping pupils relate phonemes in words to their printed symbols make this an outstanding teaching tool.

SRA Reading Laboratories (Science Research Associates).

Boxed materials complete with stories and exercises emphasizing vocabulary and comprehension are available for pupils from grades 1 through 12. Additional skills which are highlighted are rate, listening, phonics, and general word structure.

Webster Classroom Reading Clinic (Webster Division, McGraw-Hill Book Company).

There are many components in the laboratory which are designed to aid children at the elementary level in building in such areas as comprehension, sight word vocabulary, and phonics. The box contains 224 reading skill cards with reading for understanding questions; twenty copies of *Conquests in Reading* and *The Magic World of Dr. Spello*; and the book *Teachers Guide to Remedial Reading* by Dr. Kottmeyer for the teacher.

READING SERIES

Adventures in Space (Feron Publishers).

This collection of high-interest, low-readability books is for use with students who are functioning between the 2.5 and 3.5 reading levels. The series consist of four sets of books with three books to the set. The stories draw on the student's "television knowledge." The stories are short enough to allow the students to finish reading a complete selection.

Be A Better Reader Series (Prentice-Hall).

The major emphasis in this collection of books is in the area of word attack and vocabulary in the content areas of social studies, literature, biological sciences, and mathematics. Students whose instructional reading levels range from grades 4 through 12 should be able to use the volumes with much success.

Childhood of Famous Americans Series (Bobbs-Merrill).

There are over 100 biographies in this series which have been compiled for pupils who have middle-grade reading abilities but whose interests range as high as the junior-high level.

Cowboy Sam, Dan Frontier and *Sailor Jack Series* (Benefic Press).

The *Cowboy Sam* series consists of 15 books; the *Dan Frontier* group is comprised of 10 books; and the *Sailor Jack* set has 10 books. All books have kindergarten through third-grade level reading difficulty with third- through fifth-grade interest levels.

The Fitzhugh Plus Program (Allied Education Council).

This program contains nine books for work in such areas as English and mathematics. The learning program is built around the concept of repetition with the use of a *Plus* marker for noting responses. The material was developed and tested for use with students who have various learning problems.

Instant Readers (Holt, Rinehart and Winston).

These readers are for the developing student and have appeal to both the eye and ear. The books repeat and rhyme as well as interlock and accumulate words and phrases. All stories are based upon familiar cultural sequences. Through picture clues and repetition of common phrases, children are aided in reading the stories themselves.

Landmark Books (Random House).

Pupils who enjoy reading about historical events and important people should be able to use these materials. The volumes have a middle-grade reading difficulty and an upper-grade reading interest level.

New Practice Reader (Webster Publishing Company).

The major emphasis of these readers is to teach specific comprehension skills such as selecting details, differentiating between fact and opinion, and comparing word meanings. Pupils whose instructional reading levels are from 2 through 8 can use the materials profitably for the above purpose.

Pacemaker Classics (Fearon Publishers).

This series now contains five titles and is written to bring recognized functional classics within the reach of the educable mentally retarded, the slow learners, and the reluctant reader. Titles in the series include *The Jungle Book*, *The Last of The Mohicans*, *The Moonstone*, *Robinson Crusoe*, and the latest title is *Treasure Island*.

Pacemaker True Adventures (Fearon Publishers).

There are four titles in this series, with three short stories in each volume. The stories describe important events in the lives of courageous men and women, focusing on an important character trait that helped the person through trying and dangerous times. The reading levels range from 2.3 to 2.5.

Play The Game Series (Bowmar).

This collection of books is geared for grades 3 through 8 and is of the high-interest–low-vocabulary variety. The major theme in the stories is sports, and each story emphasizes life values.

Read-Aloud Books (Follett Publishing Company).

Slow-learning children who need exciting books which are written at kindergarten through third-grade levels will find these volumes useful. There are 41 books in the total program.

Sequent-A-Sets (Dexter and Westbrook).

The series consists of sets of pictures that tell a story when placed in sequential order. There are nine different sets with four pictures in each set. The materials are designed for use with children who are near the end of the kindergarten or at the beginning of the first grade.

Simplified Classics (Scott-Foresman and Company).

The main intent of this series is to provide simplified versions of famous literature selections for the slow learner and/or pupils who have reading difficulties. Reading grade level for the stories has been constructed at the fourth- to fifth-grade level with a junior-high interest level.

Specific Skill Series (Barnell Loft).

This series contains exercises in seven different skill areas at six different reading levels. The skills included are *Following Directions, Using The Context, Getting The Facts, Locating The Answer, Working With Sounds, Getting The Main Idea,* and *Drawing Conclusions.* The materials are easy to read and appeal to slow-learning children.

Teen Age Tales (D. C. Heath).

Adolescents who have below-grade reading abilities may wish to read the many stories of adventure, mystery, and action which are contained in the series. The general reading grade-level difficulty is fourth to sixth grade, with an interest grade level of from sixth through the eleventh grade.

The Young Adventures Series (Bowmar).

The reading levels of this six-book series is from fourth through sixth grade; however, they have interest levels from fourth through ninth grade and are especially suited to the slow-learning child. Subjects used in the stories are surfing, dune-buggy racing, scuba diving, snow skiing, and fire fighting. A teacher's guide is available for the materials.

Appendix A

ANNOTATED PROFESSIONAL BOOK LIST FOR TEACHERS OF SLOW LEARNING CHILDREN

The following list has been compiled from the large array of professional books which are available. Due to the extensive nature of the list, the reader will need to choose only those books which appear to meet his or her particular needs. The comments indicated reflect the general description of the various volumes and are not intended as critiques of the work.

Bernstein, Bebe: *Everyday Problems and The Child With Learning Difficulties* (New York, John Day, 1967).

This book is written to help the special child cope with everyday problem solving when he becomes an adult. Many situation problems which seem simple to the average child can mean frustration and humiliation to the child with learning difficulties. Problems such as the following are dealt with in the volume: What should you do when you ride or travel? Why do you put food in the refrigerator? Where should you play? Complete lessons for solving these problems are presented in the book.

Bernstein, Bebe: *Readiness and Reading For the Retarded Child* (New York, John Day, 1965).

Retarded children have one background experience that all share in common, the home experience. This book presents a curriculum that deals with home environments and is meaningful to the teacher of the young retarded child.

Bond, Guy L. and Tinker, Miles A.: *Reading Difficulties: Their Diagnosis and Correction*, 2nd ed. (New York, Appleton, 1967).

The primary purpose of this work is to enable teachers and clinicians to diagnose and correct reading disability cases. It is a comprehensive aid for the remedial teacher.

Bullock, Harrison: *Helping the Non-Reading Pupil in the Secondary School* (New York, Columbia, 1956).

This volume represents a specific attempt to help classroom teachers meet the needs of the nonreader by a realistic adaptation of the high school curriculum.

Cratty, Bryant J.: *Motor Activity and the Education of Retardates* (Philadelphia, Lea & Febiger, 1969).

Much of this publication places emphasis on the teaching of large and fine muscle skills. Illustrated examples of games and activities are of special value to the E.M.H. teacher. The appendix section contains examples of different tests which can be given to students.

Cushenbery, Donald C.: *Reading Improvement in the Elementary School* (West Nyack, N. Y., Parker, 1969).

The volume contains information relative to all major phases of reading and offers practical suggestions to classroom teachers for dealing with common reading instructional problems.

Cushenbery, Donald C.: *Remedial Reading in The Secondary School* (West Nyack, N. Y., Parker, 1972).

An overview of the reading procedures which should be used by all teachers is included. Teaching suggestions are listed for aiding secondary pupils in vocabulary and comprehension.

Delacato, Carl H.: *Treatment and Prevention of Reading Problems* (Springfield, Thomas, 1961).

Dr. Delacato presents a neuropsychological approach to the treatment and prevention of reading problems. The information is authoritative and useful. It is an excellent introductory book for one interested in minimal brain dysfunction.

Dupont, Henry: *Educating Emotionally Disturbed Children; Readings* (New York, Holt, 1969).

The major purpose of this volume is to introduce the classroom teacher to a clinical education approach to the emotionally disturbed child in the public schools. Clinical teaching involving screening, diagnosis, and assessment is discussed.

Durkin, Dolores: *Teaching Them to Read* (Boston, Allyn & Bacon, 1970).

This text is an attempt to combine theories of reading with

practical uses. It provides background for anyone considering a total reading program for a school by delineating what a student must know to be a better reader.

Ekwall, Eldon E.: *Locating and Correcting Reading Difficulties* (Columbus, Charles E. Merrill, 1970).

This writing is an excellent handbook for the diagnostician. Each section contains definitions of specific reading errors and possible choices for remediation.

Fallon, Berlie J. and Filgo, Dorothy J.: *Forty States Innovate to Improve School Reading Programs* (Bloomington, Ind., Phi Delta Kappa, 1970).

Descriptions of seventy-five exemplary programs in reading are included in this volume. These programs range from readiness and beginning reading through the high-school level. Appendices are included.

Farr, Roger: *Measurement and Evaluation of Reading* (New York, Harcourt, Brace and Jovanovich, 1970) .

This volume contains a collection of essays dealing with measurement and evaluation techniques in reading assessment. Section one deals with what can be evaluated. Section two gives information on practices in evaluating programs and students. Section three deals with improving classroom evaluation of student reading power. Section four outlines the procedures and problems in measuring specific reading skills. Section five gives help in estimating change and reading ability.

Figurel, J. Allen: *Reading Goals for the Disadvantaged* (Newark, Del., International Reading Association, 1970).

A collection of essays that deals with specific problems of the disadvantaged can be found in this source. It takes into consideration that background can be a causative factor of the slow learner.

Gray, William S.: *On Their Own in Reading*, revised ed. (Chicago, Scott, Foresman, 1960).

The author proceeds on the premise that students know language on the level that one should teach and that children can benefit by an analysis of word attack. A unique section on the usage of the dictionary as an aid to word perception is included.

Harris, Albert J.: *How to Increase Reading Ability*, 5th ed. (New York, McKay, 1970).

The basic characteristics of the earlier series are also encompassed in this edition. The four guiding principles are scope, balance, practicality, and clarity. This is a complete handbook for dealing with children who are reading below grade level for a multitude of reasons.

Harvat, Robert W.: *Physical Education for Children With Perceptual Motor Learning Disabilities* (Columbus, Charles E. Merrill, 1971).

This book is especially good for the physical education teacher. Group games and activities are included. Suggestions on how to schedule classes for these children are also suggested.

Haugen, T. J. and MacDonald, R. L.: *Programmed Instruction and the Education of Slow Learning Students* (Los Angeles, Remediation Associates, 1965).

The author has composed a scholarly discussion on the use of programmed instruction for the slow-learning child.

Heilman, Arthur W.: *Principles and Practices of Teaching Reading*, 2nd ed. (Columbus, Charles E. Merrill, 1967).

New developments in the field of reading are explored in this text. Chapters included deal with individualized reading, linguistics, and working with remedial readers. Principles which relate to remedial readers can easily be adapted for the slow learner.

Henderson, Richard L. and Green, Donald Ross: *Reading for Meaning in the Elementary School* (Englewood Cliffs, Prentice-Hall, 1969).

This text is a basic primary source which has been written for pre-service and in-service teachers. The first section describes what is known about the reading process. Subsequent chapters deal with learning to get meaning from print. Other chapters are devoted to analyzing meaning and learning and language and their roles in the reading process.

Howitt, Lillian C.: *Creative Techniques for Teaching the Slow Learner* (New York, Teachers Practical Press, 1964).

This is a practical handbook with specific teaching techniques for the teacher who deals with the slow learner. A special and unique section deals with curriculum adaptations. Importance of reading materials and use of audiovisual aids are other areas discussed by the author.

Humphrey, James H. and Sullivan, Dorothy D.: *Teaching Slow Learners Through Active Games* (Springfield, Thomas, 1970).

The slow learner is identified and the various types of slow learners are described in this publication. The authors feel that active involvement in learning is necessary for the slow learner. Theory and research supporting learning through games is presented and followed by over 200 examples of games to teach skills in reading, elementary-school mathematics, and elementary-school science.

Johnson, Orville G.: *Education for the Slow Learners* (Englewood Cliffs, Prentice-Hall, 1963).

This volume tries to define the problems presented by the slow learners from an educational point of view. Principles, with descriptions concerning their applications as possible approaches to solutions of problems, are presented. Various content areas such as language arts, mathematics, and science are explored in relation to the needs of slow learners.

Kaluger, George and Kolson, Clifford J.: *Reading and Learning Disabilities* (Columbus, Bell and Howell, 1969).

This text is written for the teacher of the disabled reader. It takes into consideration the diverse reasons for the nonachieving child and emphasizes different methods of instruction for different learning disabilities.

Karlin, Muriel S. and Berger, Regina: *Successful Methods for Teaching the Slow Learner* (West Nyack, N. Y., Parker, 1969).

This work is intended as a help to teachers in understanding the slow learners' problems and assisting the teacher with realistic solutions. The text stresses ingenuity and creativity in awakening children's minds. Specific ways to build success patterns for the slow learner are discussed.

Karlin, Robert: *Teaching Elementary Reading Principles and Strategies* (Chicago, Harcourt, Brace and Jovanovich, 1971).

This text was written to give teachers insights into problem areas of reading. It also seeks to demonstrate ways of improving the teaching of reading. One of the assumptions is that teachers must understand the basic rationales underlying various reading methods. Much attention is devoted to the middle grades.

Kephart, Newell C.: *The Slow Learner in the Classroom.* (Columbus, Charles E. Merrill, 1960).

This volume is a source for the classroom teacher who must work with slow learners and for the special education teacher. The book provides definitions, observations, and methods for use in the classroom. The chapters are written primarily for kindergarten and the first three grades, but the procedures could be used for older pupils if altered to provide adequate motivation.

Kolburne, Luma Louis: *Effective Education for the Mentally Retarded Child* (New York, Vantage, 1965).

The major thrust of this book is in the area of E.M.H. However, the chapter on "Borderline Classification" gives an accurate and concise description of the slow learner. Other areas of the book would be helpful as background information.

Kolstoe, Oliver and Frey, Roger M.: *A High School Work-Study Program for Mentally Subnormal Students* (Carbondale, Ill., S.I.U., 1965).

This publication is intended primarily for teachers and those who supervise work-study programs. The material would be helpful to anyone planning high school curriculum for the slow learner.

MacDonald, Robert L.: *Guidance of Parents of Slow-Learning Children* (New York, Media Press, 1966).

This small pamphlet is a good book for parents. It is arranged in a question-answer format and covers areas such as a definition of the term, *slow learner,* and the role that parents play in the education of slow learners.

McCarthy, James J. and McCarthy, Joan F.: *Learning Disabilities* (Boston, Allyn and Bacon, 1969).

This book is intended for teachers of handicapped children who are in the public school systems. The term "learning disabilities" as used in this book encompasses psychological and educational problems of the child who is normal in sensory, physical, and intellectual attributes.

Money, John: *Reading Disability: Progress and Research Needs in Dyslexia* (Baltimore, Johns Hopkins, 1962).

This collection of readings is a work that a research-minded teacher needs to own. No specific teaching suggestions are given; however, several scholarly discussions of dyslexia are included which are valuable for the general understanding of the problem.

Olson, Arthur V. and Ames, Wilbur S.: *Teaching Reading Skills in Secondary Schools: Reading* (Scranton, International Textbook, 1970).

Although this book is designed to discuss teaching of general reading skills in the high school, it is of great value to the teacher of the slow learner. Significant areas explored are reading skills in the content area and developing vocabulary and word-recognition skills.

Otto, Wayne and McMenemy, Richard A.: *Corrective and Remedial Teaching Principles and Practices* (Geneva, Ill., Houghton-Mifflin, 1966).

This book was written as an attempt to eradicate illiteracy among normal school-age children who have no vision or hearing problems and are normal mentally. Many of the sections deal with the slow learner.

Otto, Wayne and Ford, David.: *Teaching Adults to Read* (Geneva, Ill., Houghton-Mifflin, 1967).

This source presents many approaches to teaching adults to read. The authors realize that adults as well as children can not be taught by a one-method approach. This book serves as a guide to materials, methods, and ideas.

Ravenette, A. T.: *Dimensions of Reading Difficulties* (New York, Pergamon, 1968).

The major purpose of this writing is to provide a common language for different professions to use when dealing with reading difficulties. All factors including organic, environmental, educational, and psychological are included. Critical stages of human development as they relate to reading are also discussed.

Riessman, Frank.: *Helping the Disadvantaged Pupil to Learn More Easily* (Englewood Cliffs, N. J. Prentice-Hall, 1966).

This volume has portions which both the classroom teacher and administrator can use. Of special interest are chapters concerning remediation of weaknesses, selection of materials, and development of interest on the part of parents in the program.

Rosenzweig, Louis E. and Long, Julia.: *Understanding and Teaching the Dependent Retarded Child* (Darien, Conn., Educational Publishing, 1960).

Five major skill areas are covered by the authors: self-help, social, motor, academic, and vocational. The teaching approach is designed to stress developmental blocks of a child's growth pattern for any child who deviates from the norm in social, emotional, or physical patterns. This is a good source to recommend to parents.

Roucek, Joseph S.: *The Slow Learner* (New York, Philosophical Library, 1969).

This collection of reading deals with various aspects of the slow learner. A section of interest is that dealing with motivation of underachievers and the disadvantaged in our society. This is an excellent reference for one seeking background information in this area.

Schell, Leo M. and Burns, Paul C.: *Remedial Reading, An Anthology of Sources* (Boston, Allyn & Bacon, 1968).

This is an anthology of remedial reading articles encompassing causative factors and identifying, diagnosing, and remediating reading problems. Also included are principles of instruction, instructional procedures, and instructional materials. A special section deals with readers with emotional problems.

Schubert, Delwyn and Torgerson, Theodore L.: *Improving Reading in the Elementary School* (Dubuque, Iowa: Brown, 1968).

Individualized instruction in reading, and analyzing difficulties in word recognition and word analysis are emphasized in this set of materials. The appendix section is informative. Reading games and exercises are suggested in addition to the other information.

Smith, Henry P. and Dechant, Emerald: *Psychology in Teaching Reading.* (Englewood Cliffs, Prentice-Hall, 1961).

This text provides teachers with a basic understanding of the psychological implications in the reading process. The authors attempt to organize facts concerning reading behavior. The book gives insight into problems that are encountered by retarded readers.

Smith, James A.: *Creative Teaching of Reading and Literature in the Elementary School* (Boston, Allyn & Bacon, 1969).

Emphasis on creativity in reading is a strong point in this work. Several good methods that could be adapted for use with the slow learner are included. The book is easy to read, and useful chapter bibliographies are also included.

Smith, Robert M.: *Teacher Diagnosis of Educational Difficulties* (Columbus, Charles E. Merrill, 1969).

The primary function of Smith's volume is to awaken educators to the idea that variance of children's ability can be dealt with effectively by educational programs when teachers attain skills necessary in assessing those abilities.

Smith, Robert M.: *Clinical Teaching Methods of Instruction for the Retarded* (New York, McGraw-Hill, 1968).

The author uses a systematic theoretical method for dealing with the retarded student. The major premise of instruction is that strengths and weaknesses must be identified in order to formulate a child's educational program. The author stresses psychological and scientific research methods for dealing with the retarded child.

Spache, George D.: *Reading in the Elementary School* (Boston, Allyn & Bacon, 1964).

Presented here is a unique approach to elementary-teacher training of the reading teacher. The author realizes the problem of the inexperienced teacher in deciding which method to use. Dr. Spache favors the eclectic method for the beginning teacher and explains why in his book.

Stauffer, Russell G.: *The Language Experience Approach to the Teaching of Reading* (New York, Harper and Row, 1970).

This source has especially good ideas for using the language-experience approach with slow learners. A method for developing a sequential body of skills through the language experience approach is discussed. Of interest to the teacher of the slow learner is the chapter entitled, "Special Uses of the Language Experience Approach."

Steimer, Violette G. and Pond, Roberta Evott: *Finger Play Fun* (Columbus, Charles E. Merrill, 1970).

This book is designed to be used with students who are 2 to 6 years old. Each chapter is organized around a special theme. Activity poems are used.

Taba, Hilda and Elkins, Deborah: *Teaching Strategies for the Culturally Disadvantaged* (Chicago, Rand-McNally, 1966).

A series of sequences of curriculum teaching for culturally deprived students is found in this source. It is intended for teachers and other educational workers concerned with preadolescents.

Tiedt, Sidney W. (Ed.): *Teaching the Disadvantaged Child.* (New York, Oxford, 1968).

Tiedt has collected a number of chapters which are designed to broaden the knowledge of those seeking to deal with the disadvantaged child. Divergent points of view are represented. The book gives both theory and practice.

Tinker, Miles A.: *Bases for Effective Reading* (Minneapolis, University of Minnesota Press, 1965).

This text is divided into five parts. Parts three and four are particularly valuable for the teacher of the slow learner.

Wallen, Carl J.: *Word Attack Skills in Reading* (Columbus, Charles E. Merrill, 1969).

Dr. Wallen has developed a process for teaching word-attack skills with illustrated lessons to help the teacher apply these processes in the classroom. Special attention is given to interaction between teacher and student and to classroom diagnosis of word-attack skill needs.

Waugh, Kenneth W. and Bush, Wilma J.: *Diagnosing Learning Disorders* (Columbus, Charles E. Merrill, 1971).

Twelve of the most common learning behaviors are discussed in this publication. Descriptions of diagnostic tests and interpretation of tests are included. A good glossary of learning-disorder terms is also included. It would be beneficial to teachers at all levels.

Wilson, Robert M.: *Diagnostic and Remedial Reading for Classroom and Clinic* (Columbus, Charles E. Merrill, 1972).

This volume attempts to help the classroom teacher adapt and apply various aspects of diagnosis and remediation. The principles involved are those of the clinic as well as the real situation of the classroom. An excellent chapter on the role of the parent of the problem reader may also be found.

Young, Milton A.: *Teaching Children With Special Learning Needs: A Problem Solving Approach* (New York, John Day, 1967).

Dr. Young presents a plan for diagnostic teaching in the classroom which involves the analysis of the learning environment. The book includes philosophy and practice that can be applied by teachers. Especially informative is the taxonomy of needs of these special children and the numerous exercises which can meet these needs.

Appendix B

PRIMARY-LEVEL LANGUAGE-ARTS
MATERIALS FOR SLOW LEARNERS

The primary curriculum for slow-learning children is basically a readiness program. As such, the program is largely non-academic.

The teacher's major responsibility is to develop a strong readiness program. This should provide experiences which will enable the child to make acceptable academic gains in intermediate and junior-high classes. Formal reading experiences should begin when the child has sufficient background for the reading act; however, information reading, using experience charts and other materials, should be a part of each teacher's lessons plans.

The reader should consult Appendix E for the names and addresses of publishers. Appreciation is extended to Mrs. Charlene Lenz of the Area 13 Ed. Dist. for permission to reprint the information in Appendices B, C, and D.

Publisher	Title	Description
Follett	The Parkinson Program for Special Children, Rev. Stage I Reading Readiness Kit, Rev.	A complete kit—teacher's manual plus materials for 15 children; excellent for the youngest children M.A. 3 and 4, for directed work. Developed specifically for EMR's.
Follett	The Parkinson Program for Special Children, Rev. Stage II—Reading Readiness Workbooks	Readiness materials for small group work under direction. Can follow materials listed above or be a part of general readiness for M.A. 4+. Developed specifically for EMR children.

Publisher	*Title*	*Description*
Follett	The Frostig Developmental Program in Visual Perception Pictures and Patterns, Beginning, Intermediate, Advanced	These three workbooks contain most of the materials incorporated in the Frostig sheets.
Follett	The Frostig Visual Perception Materials	Study sheets for use by small groups in a directed situation. Excellent if used as suggested.
American Guidance Services	Peabody Language Development Kit; Primary (MA 3–5)	Contains many manipulative items to encourage language; with teacher's manual.
American Guidance Services	Peabody Language Development Kit No. 1 (MA 4½–6½)	Language stimulation for small groups by means of manipulative items and stimulus cards.
Continental Press	Useful Language, Level I, Level II, Level III; Visual Motor Skills, Level I; Visual Discrimination, Level I; Thinking Skills, Level I	Duplication materials for use with small groups in directed study lessons.
John Day	Now I Look Now I Read	Readiness materials for small group work.
Harcourt, Brace and Jovanovich	Let's Talk and Listen Let's Talk and Write	Beginning communication skills.
Field Educational Publications	Words for Writing, A to Z Spellers	Beginning experiences in written communication.
Charles E. Merrill	Visual Experiences for Creative Growth, Developmental Activity Series Units I and II, Units III and IV, Units V and VI	Sixty large study prints which should be used sequentially. Motor coordination and physical activities stressed. Social-emotional concepts. Language skills.

Publisher	Title	Description
Judy Company	Sequees, Series 4, 6, 12, All Titles	For directed small group readiness.
Judy Company	Stick-O-Mats	For readiness activities in developing form perception and language concepts.
Gary Lawson	Fun With Us Ride With Us Play With Us	For directed work with advanced readiness group.
Scott, Foresman	Learn to Listen, Speak and Write Series Level 1-1 Level 1-2	Teachers' edition—particularly helpful. Beginning experiences in written communication.
Scott, Foresman	Linguistic Block Series The First Rolling Reader	Mature primary children will enjoy working with these under direction.
Scott, Foresman	We Read Pictures We Read More Pictures Before We Read	Teachers' edition—readiness skills with small groups.
E. C. Seale	I Learn to Write Kindergarten Book One	For teacher use. Stimulates written language with emphasis on words.
Stanwix House	Readiness Materials Steps to Reading	Work sheets to be used, under direction.
Stanwix House	The "Getting Ready to Read" Workbook The "Our Dog" Workbook	Readiness material, approaching level for reading.
Stanwix House	Functional Basic Readers About King About Mary and Bill About Friends About Fun and Play About Things at Home (Other titles suggested at other age levels.)	A basic series for EMR children. For directed study with small groups.
Follett	I Want to Learn	Charts, activity books and teachers' guide to develop readiness skills.

Publisher	*Title*	*Description*
Encyclopedia Britannica Press	Language Experiences in Reading	Programmed series for beginning reading and writing.
Holt	Sounds of the Home, Very First Words	Single copies.
Follett	Picture Dictionary	Two or three copies.
Little, Brown	What If for My Birthday?	To be read by teacher to group-language stimulation.
Holt	Kinder Owls	Individual copies, picture and story books. This set includes 20 books in language literature, arithmetic, social studies, and science areas.
Follett	Pre-Reading Read Aloud Books	Library books (45) to develop readiness skills.
Random House	Dr. Seuss Series	To be read by teacher to group.
Garrard	The Happy Bears	Readiness and beginning reading book and game.
Primary Educational	Non-oral Reading Series	Picture charts, word cards and wall charts.
Harper and Row	School Readiness Treasure Chest	Library books (36) to develop readiness in language arts, arithmetic, and social studies.
McGraw-Hill	The Headstart Book of Looking and Listening of Knowing and Naming of Thinking and Imagining	Games, stories and rhymes to extend readiness skills.
Follett	Listen-Hear Books	Six books with emphasis on auditory discrimination.
Appleton	Matrix Games	Games to develop language skills.
Mafex	Training Fun with Writing Book I and II	Begins with letters and moves into words and sentences.

INTERMEDIATE-LEVEL LANGUAGE ARTS MATERIALS FOR SLOW LEARNERS

Publisher	*Title*	*Description*
Benefic	Butternut Bill Series	Reading levels Primary–3.
Melmont	Easy to Read Books	Reading levels 1–3.
Melmont	Good Times Books	Reading levels 1–3.
Holt	Sounds of Language Readers	Collection of poems, stories and articles, with teachers' manuals.
Benefic	Animal Adventure Series	Reading levels Preprimary–3.
Benefic	Button Family Series	Reading levels Preprimary–1.
Random House	Beginner Books	Reading levels Preprimary–2.
Follett	Beginning to Read Series	Reading levels 2–3.
Benefic	Easy to Read Books	Reading levels 2–3.
Garrard	True Stories	Reading levels 2–3.
Garrard	Folklore Stories	Reading levels 2–3.
Benefic	What Is It Series	Reading levels 2–3.

Appendix D

SENIOR HIGH-LEVEL LANGUAGE ARTS MATERIALS FOR SLOW LEARNERS

Publisher	Title	Description
Arthur C. Croft	Educator's Washington Dispatch Home and Family Life Series "A Day With the Brown Family" "Making a Good Living" "The Browns at School" "The Browns and Their Neighbors"	Written for adult illiterates. These books provide material for EMR who arrives at senior high without measurable reading skills.
Exceptional Products	Signs of Everyday Life	Use with groups.
Globe	English on the Job, Book 1 and 2	Part I of each book provides good review of functional English.
Pierson	Lawson, Gary: Newspaper Reading	Pupil resource in English; should be related to use of the local newspaper.
Teaching Aids	Doorways to Employment, Two-pad set	Introductory form for job applications.
S.R.A.	The Job Ahead, Level I	Provides meaningful reading experiences relative to adult life.
Steck-Vaughn	I Want to Read and Write Learning and Writing English, Book I and II Adult Reader	For directed-study supplemental use, small groups.
Stanwix	Functional Basic Reading Series	For directed study with small groups. Content

Publisher	Title	Description
	"Off to Work" (Grade 9 or 10) "Calomba's Place" (Grade 9 or 10)	can be related to occupational adequacy, citizenship responsibility.
Ginn	Help Yourself to Read, Write, and Spell	Adult-interest words related to home, shop, and sports.
Allied	Mott Basic Language Skills Program 300	Sequential program designed for adolescents.
Reader's Digest	Reader's Digest Reading Skill Builders Level 1-6	Content is appropriate for older adolescent; skill development in word recognition and comprehension.
Noble and Noble	Write Your Own Letters	Example of personal and business letters.
Globe	English on the Job, Book I and II	Part I of each book provides good review.
Globe	Vocational English, Book I and II	Good teacher-pupil reference.
Holt	Language In Your Life, Book 1 and 2	Paperback, short lessons.
Ginn	Our American Language	Good review of grammar is simplified.
Harper	An Oral Language Practice Book	
Harper	Spoken Drills and Tests in English	Based on ear training.
Harper	Laugh and Learn Grammar	Written at approximately fourth and fifth grade level with humorous illustrations.
Follett	The Turner Livingston Communications Series	Emphasizes the Communication facets in daily living (6 books, 87¢ each).
Follett	Success in Language and Literature A/B	Teacher resource.
Scholastic	Scope Reading Skills	Titles such as Word Puzzles & Mysteries, Jobs in Your Future (75¢ each).

Publisher	*Title*	*Description*
Follett	Turner Livingston Reading Series	Titles include Money You Spend, Jobs You Get, Person You Are (6 books, 87¢ each).
Follett	Turner Guidance Series	Six books, 87¢ each.
	Newspaper Reading	A worktext ($1.50).
Lawson	Oral Language Practice	
Follett	Vocational Reading Series	Titles include Practical Nurse, Auto Mechanic, Department Store Worker ($1.26 each).
Follett	Play It Cool English	$1.23.

Appendix E

LIST OF PUBLISHERS AND THEIR ADDRESSES

T his list contains the addresses of publishing companies which have been mentioned in this book.

Allen Company, 4200 Arbutus Court, Heyward, California 94542.

Allied Education Council, Distribution Center, Box 78, Gallen, Michigan.

Allyn & Bacon, Inc., Rockleigh, New Jersey 07647.

American Association Health, Physical Education & Recreation, 1201 16th Street, N.W., Washington, D.C. 20036.

American Book Company, 55 Fifth Avenue, New York, New York 10003.

American Education Publications, Education Center, Columbus, Ohio 43216.

American Guidance, Inc., Publishers' Building, Circle Pines, Minnesota 55014.

American Library Association, 50 East Huron Street, Chicago, Illinois 60611.

Audio-Visual Research, 1502 8th Street, S.E., Waseca, Minnesota 56093.

Bailey Film Associates, 11559 Santa Monica Boulevard, Los Angeles, California 90025.

Bantam Books, Inc., 666 5th Avenue, New York, New York 10019.

Barnell Loft, Ltd., 111 South Centre Ave., Rockville Centre, New York 10016.

Behavioral Research Laboratories, Box 577, Palo Alto, California 94302.

Bell & Howell Company, Audio-Visual Products Division, 7100 McCormick Blvd., Chicago, Illinois 60645.

Benefic Press, 10300 W. Roosevelt Road, Westchester, Illinois 60153.

Benton Review Publishing Company, Fowler, Indiana 47944.

Bobbs-Merrill Company, 4300 W. 62nd Street, Indianapolis, Indiana 46268.

Bowmar, 622 Rodier Drive, Glendale, California 91201.

California Test Bureau (A Division of McGraw-Hill Book Company), Del Monte Research Park, Monterey, California 93940.

Cenco Educational Aids, 2600 S. Kostner Ave., Chicago, Illinois 60623.

Children's Press, 1224 W. Van Buren, Chicago, Illinois 60607.

Civic Education Service, 1733 K Street, N.W., Washington, D.C. 20006.

Clinical Psychology Publishing Company, Brandon, Vermont 05733.

Committee on Diagnostic Reading Tests, Mountain Home, North Carolina 28758.

F. E. Compton, 425 N. Michigan Avenue, Chicago, Illinois 60611.

Constructive Playthings, 1040 East 85th Street, Kansas City, Missouri 64131.

Continental Press, Elizabethtown, Pennsylvania 17022.

Coronet Films, 65 E. South Water Street, Chicago, Illinois 60601.

Creative Playthings, Inc., Princeton, New Jersey 08540.

Cuisenaire Company of America, Inc., 9 Elm Avenue, Mount Vernon, New York 10550.

The John Day Company, Inc., 62 West 45th Street, New York, New York 10036.

Dell Publishing Company, 750 Third Avenue, New York, N. Y. 10017.

Developmental Learning Materials, 3505 N. Ashland Avenue, Chicago, Illinois 60657.

Developmental Reading Distributors, 1944 Sheridan Avenue, Laramie, Wyoming 82070.

Dexter and Westbrook, Ltd., 111 South Centre Avenue, Rockville Centre, New York 11571.

Doubleday & Company, Inc., Garden City, New York 11530.

The Economics Press, Inc., P. O. Box 480, Montclair, New Jersey 07042.

The Economy Company, 1901 No. Walnut, Oklahoma City, Oklahoma 73105.

Educational Developmental Laboratories, 824 Pulaski Road, Huntington, New York 11743.

Educational Progress Corporation, 8538 East 41st Street, Tulsa, Oklahoma 74145.

Educational Record Sales, 153 Chambers Street, New York, New York 10007.

Educational Service, Inc., P. O. Box 112, Benton Harbor, Michigan 49022.

Educator's Publishing Service, 75 Moulton Street, Cambridge, Massachusetts 02138.

Encyclopedia Britannica Educational Corporation, 425 N. Michigan Avenue, Chicago, Illinois 60611.

Encyclopedia Britannica Press, Inc., 425 North Michigan Avenue, Chicago, Illinois 60611.

Encyclopedia International, School and Library Division, 575 Lexington Avenue, New York, N. Y. 10022.

Exceptional Products Corporation, P. O. Box 6374, Minneapolis, Minnesota 55423.

Eye Gate House, Inc., 146-01 Archer Avenue, Jamaica, New York 11435.

Fawcett Publications, Inc., 67 West 44th Street, New York, New York 10036.

Fearon Publishers, 2165 Park Boulevard, Palo Alto, California 94306.

Field Educational Publications, Inc., 609 Mission Street, San Francisco, California 94105.

Field Enterprises Educational Corporation, Merchandise Mart, Chicago, Illinois 60654.

The Finney Company, 3350 Gorham Avenue, Minneapolis, Minnesota 55426.

Follett Educational Corporation, Customer Service Center, P. O. Box 5705, Chicago, Illinois 60680.

F.O.R.E. Communications Management Group, 2020 R. Street, N.W., Washington, D.C. 20009.

Funk & Wagnalls Company, Inc., 380 Madison Avenue, New York, New York 10017.

Garrard Press, 510 N. Hickory Street, Champaign, Illinois 61820.

Gill Company, 125 Second Avenue, Waltham, Massachusetts 02154.

Globe Book Company, Inc., 175 Fifth Avenue, New York, New York 10010.

Golden Press, Inc., 850 Third Avenue, New York, New York 10022.

Grolier, Inc., 575 Lexington Ave., New York, New York 10022.

Grolier Educational Corp., 845 Third Avenue, New York, New York 10022.

Grosset & Dunlap, 51 Madison Avenue, New York, New York 10010.

The Gryphon Press, Highland Park, New Jersey 08904.

E. M. Hale and Company, 1201 S. Hastings Way, Eau Claire, Wisconsin 54702.

C. S. Hammond & Company, 515 Valley Street, Maplewood, New Jersey 07040.

Harcourt, Brace and Jovanovich, 757 3rd Avenue, New York, New York 10017.

Harper & Row, 49 East 33rd Street, New York, New York 10016.

Hayes School Publishing Company, 321 Pennwood Avenue, Wilkinsburg, Pennsylvania 15221.

D. C. Heath and Company, A Division of Raytheon Education Co., 2700 North Richardt Avenue, Indianapolis, Indiana 46219.

Holt, Rinehart and Winston, 383 Madison Avenue, New York, New York 10017.

Houghton-Mifflin Company, 1900 Botovia Ave., Geneva, Illinois 60134.

Imperial Productions, Inc., 247 West Court St., Kankakee, Illinois 60901.

Initial Teaching Alphabet Publications, Inc., 20 East 46th Street, New York, New York 10017.

Instructo Products, 1635 North 55th Street, Philadelphia, Pennsylvania 19131.

The Judy Company, 310 North Second Street, Minneapolis, Minnesota 55401.

Junior Literary Guild, 9 Rockefeller Plaza, New York, New York 10020.

Kenworthy Educational Service, Inc., Box 3031, Buffalo, New York 14205.

Laidlaw Brothers (A Division of Doubleday and Company), 36 Chatham Road, Summit, New Jersey 07901.

Laidlaw Brothers, Publishers, River Forest, Illinois 60305.

Language Research Associates, 950 E. 59th Street, Chicago, Illinois.

Laubach Publishing Company, Box 131, Syracuse, New York 13210.

Gary Lawson, 9488 Sara Street, Elks Grove, California 95624.

Learning Corporation of America, 711 Fifth Avenue, New York, New York 10022.

Learning Materials, Inc., 425 N. Michigan Ave., Chicago, Illinois 60611.

Learning Research Associates, 1501 Broadway, New York, New York 10036.

Learning Through Seeing, Inc., Sunland, California 91040.

J. B. Lippincott Company, Educational Publishing Division, East Washington Square, Philadelphia, Pennsylvania 19105.

Lyons and Carnahan, 407 East 25th Street, Chicago, Illinois 60616.

The MacMillan Company, 434 South Wabash Avenue, Chicago, Illinois 60605.

Mafex Associates, Box 519, Johnstown, Pennsylvania 15907.

McCormick Mathers Publishing Company, 300 Pike Street, Cincinnati, Ohio 45202.

Melmont Publishers, Inc., 310 South Racine Avenue, Chicago, Illinois 60607.

G. & C. Merriam Company, 47 Federal Street, Springfield, Mass. 01101.

Charles E. Merrill Books, Inc., 1300 Alum Creek Drive, Columbus, Ohio 43216.

Mid America, 1224 West Van Buren Street, Chicago, Illinois 60607.

New Readers Press, Box 131, Syracuse, New York 13210.

Noble & Noble Publishers Inc., 750 Third Avenue, New York, New York 10017.

Open Court Publishing Company, P. O. Box 399, LaSalle, Illinois 61301.

F. A. Owen Publishing Company, Instructor Park, Dansville, New York 14437.

The Oxford Book Company, 71 Fifth Avenue, New York, New York 10003.

Parker Publishing Company, Inc., West Nyack, New York 10994.

Pierson Trading Company, 6109 Burns Way, Sacramento, California 95824.

Play 'N Talk Phonics, P. O. Box 18804, Oklahoma City, Oklahoma.

Porter-Sargent Publisher, 11 Beacon Street, Boston, Massachusetts 02108.

Prentice-Hall, Inc., Englewood Cliffs, New Jersey 07632.

Primary Educational Service, 1243 West 79th Street, Chicago, Illinois 60620.

Pruett Press, Inc., Boulder, Colorado 80302.

Psychological Test Corporation, 304 E. 45th Street, New York, New York 10017.

Quality Educational Development, Inc., Washington, D.C.

Rand-McNally, P. O. Box 7600, Chicago, Illinois 60690.

Random House, 457 Madison Avenue, New York, New York 10022.

Reader's Digest Services, Inc., Educational Division, Pleasantville, New York 10570.

Frank E. Richards, 1453 Main Street, Phoenix, New York 13135.

Scholastic Magazines, Englewood Cliffs, New Jersey 07632.

Science Research Associates, Inc., 259 E. Erie Street, Chicago, Illinois 07632.

Scott, Foresman and Company, 1900 East Lake, Glenview, Illinois 60025.

E. C. Seale and Co., Inc., 1053 East 54th Street, Indianapolis, Indiana 46220.

Silver-Burdett Company, Box 362, Morristown, New Jersey 07960.

Society for Visual Education, 1345 Diversey Parkway, Chicago, Illinois 60614.

Stanwix House, Inc., 3020 Chartiers Avenue, Pittsburgh, Pennsylvania 15204.

The Steck-Vaughn Company, P. O. Box 2028, Austin, Texas 78767.

Teachers College Press, Columbia University, 525 West 120th Street, New York, New York 10027.

Teaching Aids (Division of A. Daigger & Company), 159 West Kinzie Street, Chicago, Illinois 60610.

Teaching Resources, Inc., 100 Boylston Street, Boston, Massachusetts 02116.

Tools for Education, Inc., Burlington, Wisconsin 53105.

Fern Tripp, 2035 East Sierra Valley, Dinuba, California 93618.

United States Government Printing Office, Superintendent of Documents, Washington, D.C. 20402.

University of Illinois Press, Urbana, Illinois 61801.

Webster Division, McGraw-Hill Book Company, Manchester Road, Manchester, Missouri 63011.

Albert Whitman and Company, 560 West Lake Street, Chicago, Illinois 60606.

Xerox Corporation, Curriculum Programs, 600 Madison Avenue, New York, New York 10022.

AUTHOR INDEX

SUBJECT INDEX

A

Analysis of Learning Potential, 50

B

Background, experiential and educational, 88
Beery-Buktenica Developmental Test of Visual-Motor Integration, 23
Behavior modification, 116
Behavior modification, applied, 118
Botel Reading Inventory, 20, 49, 71

C

California Phonics Survey, 20, 72
Chicago Non-Verbal Examination, 50
Commercial tests, 49
  descriptions of, 49
  group survey reading tests, 49
  individual diagnostic, 50
  psychological, 50, 51
Comprehension, 55
  construction of program for slow learner, 86
  evaluating abilities in, 97
  necessary skills for, 91–95
  role in reading program, 89
  skill development of for slow learner, 86, 90
Comprehensive Tests of Basic Skills, 49
Context clues, 79
  exercises for building competencies, 80
  nature and use of, 79

D

D. A. T. Verbal Reasoning, Numerical Ability, and Abstract Reasoning Test, 50
Detroit Beginning First Grade Intelligence Test, Revised, 50
Diagnostic Reading Scales, 21, 50, 72

Dictionary,
  lessons for teaching skills in use of, 83
  use as word attack tool, 81
Directions, following, 93
Disadvantaged,
  definition of, 11
  learning problems of, 12
Dolch Basic Sight Word Test, 57, 58
Doren Diagnostic Test, 71
Durrell Analysis of Reading Difficulty, 21, 50, 72, 97

E

Educable mentally retarded child, learning problems of, 4
Emotionally disturbed
  definition of, 9
  learning problems of, 10
Evaluation, 47
  construction and use of teacher-made tests, 47
  guidelines for using test data, 63
  kinds of instruments, 48
  reasons for, 47
Evaluative instruments, kinds of, 48
Expectancy, level of, 52
Experiential background, 88

F

First Grade Screening Test, 23, 51
Frostig Developmental Test of Visual Perception, 105, 109
Frustration reading level, 56

G

Gates-MacGinitie Reading Tests, 49
Gates-McKillop Reading Diagnostic Tests, 50, 97
Gilmore Oral Reading Test, 50
Graphing, 119